CONTENTS

D1471992

CHAPTER ONE

HALF A POUND OF TUPPENNY RICE

Jane Castle, my paternal grandmother, was brought up on hard work and was 'Yorkshire' through and through. Her father, Samuel Castle, lived in a weaver's cottage in a little rural West Riding village. Sam worked a loom in an upstairs room, while his wife busied herself on one downstairs. They worked not by the clock, but by the daylight; from crack of dawn until dusk forced them to stop.

Although they toiled many hours daily, they were contented. They were their own master and mistress, and if there happened to be a cricket match on the neighbouring green, they would down tools and spend a pleasant couple of hours in the open air. Going away for a holiday in the late 1800s was never even considered, so country folk took their amusements where they could; a picnic, a walk, reading a book under a shady tree, or by the light of an oil lamp in winter.

Then there was chapel, and the social life it afforded. It was at chapel that Samuel Castle's daughter, Jane, met John Taylor, a grocer's assistant. In due course they married, and set up home in a little low decker – a small, terraced dwelling on one level – on the outskirts of Huddersfield. John became a grocer and businessman in his own right through a stroke of bad luck.

Born in 1865, John, who was to become my grandfather, was an honest, upright, hard-working and trustworthy young man. In what little leisure time he had, he enjoyed going to chapel, reading the Bible, and also Charles Dickens. Nevertheless, times

Deighton chapel, now demolished

were hard. (Is there ever a time when they aren't?) So through no fault of his own, the day came when the young husband was sacked. This story would have been very different if he hadn't been! Such are the vagaries of life: the twists, turns and circumstances we find ourselves in, and how we resolve them, and the varying pathways we decide to follow which alter the course of our lives and those of our yet unborn children.

At this difficult period, there was a young baby, Annie, to provide for. There was no time for delay. John took leave of the grocery establishment on a Saturday teatime. First thing Monday morning saw him taking the first steps to becoming John Taylor, grocer and provision merchant. There wasn't much furniture in the little home, but there was a trestle table which John pulled into the front window overlooking the road. On it he displayed his first commodity – half a pound of best butter. Then, in his best pepper-and-salt suit, and with a large wicker basket over his arm, he strode down to town and called in at wholesaler Cooper and Webb's. Would they kindly allow him credit on his first lot of grocery orders? He promised that if they would, he would continue to deal with them when he became proprietor of a prosperous grocery concern.'

Impressed with his obvious trustworthiness and eagerness to succeed against all odds, they agreed. John, light of heart, walked to the 'posh' end of town and knocked on the doors of large stone houses. Could he count on their valuable support to patronize John Taylor for future grocery orders? He would guarantee personal attention, prompt deliveries, and the very best groceries to be found. Soon he had a list of prospective customers. He hurried home, bursting into the little home exultantly.

'I'm in business!' he announced. 'We won't starve now, or have to grovel to relations for a loaf of bread or milk for the baby.'

Next morning Jane found herself in charge of another half a pound of best butter on the trestle table. It was for sale, as the big cardboard notice stated. John set off to deliver his first orders.

When John was absolutely sure that borrowing money for building a proper shop and attached house was a feasible proposition, he decided on a plot of land adjoining the fields. Everything was to be of the best quality. Foundations were dug deep, and the couple watched every step of the construction of Central Stores, as they decided to name it, from the low decker across the road. It took shape slowly but surely, built out of yellow, best Yorkshire sandstone. Two large display windows took their places either side of the shop door. A gas lamp situated on the pavement lit up the square in the front of the shop, where future generations of children would congregate to play 'Puss, Puss, Come to My Corner' and other games in its friendly glow on autumn and winter evenings.

With the outer structure completed, next came the excitement of the interior furnishings. Long before the era of fitted wardrobes, the far side of the living-kitchen behind the shop boasted large open shelves with deep drawers below. Rising from floor to ceiling, they were always referred to as 'The Fittings'. They held trays of bread and teacakes, and when Jane branched out into selling drapery, as well as groceries, the drawers were used for storing piles of combinations – 'combs' for short – those abominations with a slit at the front to enable the wearer to use the lavatory with ease, striped working mens' shirts, blouses, stockings, and other unmentionables. Packets of Mené sanitary towels were hidden away right up at the top of 'The Fittings' and never mentioned outright by name, the item always being written down on a slip of paper which was handed to Grandma.

John and Jane Taylor, who set up the shop

Dark brown Anaglypta decorated the living-kitchen walls, and a black Yorkshire range provided the only heating downstairs. There were open fires in the front room above the shop and back bedrooms, so coal had to be carried from the cellar up two flights of stairs.

Waist-high bins were installed down one side of the shop itself for flour – one for white, the other for brown – sugar and hen corn. How relaxing it was to run one's fingers through that smooth, honey-gold corn, or, in idle moments, to make patterns in the flour with the big oval-shaped scoops.

A solid mahogany counter proudly awaited its first customers, while behind it were neat rows of tiny drawers, each drawer showing the name of its contents on a gilt-edged label. What treasures there were! Whole nutmegs (none of your ready-powdered stuff then; half the pleasure of making a rice pudding was in grating a nutmeg over it, with sometimes a bit of finger skin being grated into it by mistake as well), turkey rhubarb, ginger, Gregory Powders, sulphur and brimstone, lots of herbs (camomile, mint, hyssop, marjoram), liquorice powder and

Beecham's Powders. Shelves continued to the ceiling, housing all manner of things. Bottles of Indian brandy, castor oil, jars of Vaseline, tins of Zambuck and sticks of hard, jet-black 'Spanish' (liquorice) which was kept wrapped in yellow leaves. Many customers became completely addicted to it. A pint pot of 'Spanish' juice could be seen in many a home, tucked away in a corner of the fireplace. Boiling water had to be poured over a stick, and it was then ready 'for a sup' whenever the bowels needed a bit of assistance.

Twist – brown, flecked, aromatic – lay coiled in flat, snake-like contortions in a tin box by the cigarette shelf. A special sharp knife was kept alongside to nip off the half ounces. It was usually bought by men on their way home after a hard day in the mill or dyeworks.

Open shelves beneath the counter housed packets of Acdo washing powder, Rinso, starch, Dolly Blue, and donkey stones for scouring doorsteps (a regular buy on Friday mornings when housewives were preparing for the weekend). It wasn't an unusual sight to see varying shapes and sizes of Yorkshire posteriors hanging on for dear life out of sash windows up the road from the shop, while their respective owners energetically swished wash leathers over the windowpanes. Also on the shelves were tins of Brasso and Silvo, the soft newness of yellow dusters, skipping-ropes, whips and tops, packets of chalk and marbles, shuttlecocks, and brand-new boxes of fireworks kept beneath the counter until Mischief Night was over.

From the shop ceiling hung lethal-looking iron hooks where rolls of ham and bacon swung.

Heavy round marble containers were positioned in a recess to house butter, lard and huge cheeses. The wooden boxes which the cheeses were delivered in were pounced upon with glee when empty and used for covering the young shoots of rhubarb out in the back garden.

John established himself in a business that was to flourish through two world wars, all from one half-pound of butter in that little low decker house, after getting 'the sack'. Had there been such panaceas as family allowance to lessen the worry about his baby starving, he might well not have had the same impetus to make a go of the project.

CHAPTER TWO

THE JAM FACTORY

Small, one-man businesses were flourishing all over the country at the turn of the century. There was Tripey Joe, who went round the village selling tripe every Friday at 2*d* per quarter pound, and the Hot Pea Man whose two penn'orths filled a great big jug. Another fellow began selling fish and chips in a wooden hut, but some of the more choosy villagers vowed they'd never patronize him – they'd seen him spit into the fat.

Not all were as scrupulous about hygiene as John and Jane. Out of his first small profits, while still operating from the low decker, John bought a pair of shiny brass weighing scales. In those days there was no hire purchase. In any case, the couple didn't believe in getting anything they couldn't pay for; at least not until there were tangible signs that a business would flourish.

One great asset to the success of the new venture was the fields nearby, where John's brother, William, grew soft fruits and acres of rhubarb. When not busy serving customers, the couple were boiling fruit and bottling jams in the tiny scullery at the back. Later, a small stone building – 'The Jam Factory' as it was pretentiously called – was constructed on the opposite side of the road, while the main shop was being built. Jane was soon energetically scalding out jars brought along by customers, and in no time at all the 'Factory' was a hive of industry. Jane, in long black dress covered with starched white pinafore, was at the centre of proceedings, boiling up different combinations of fruits in big brass pans. The couple were always up at dawn in summertime and went into the fields accompanied by their little dog Punch (a look-alike of the dog that featured in later years on

Grandma Taylor in the doorway of the shop, with Punch

His Master's Voice records). Punch also acted as the burglar alarm for the shop. The fruit was carried back in large wooden trays. After breakfast the jars were scalded out again in the 'peggy tub', then labels pasted on to them with a mixture of flour and water. Finally the names of the preserves were neatly printed on in ink.

There was such an abundance of succulent fruits that Jane eventually couldn't cope alone. The couple were now selling home-made jams and preserves to enthusiastic wholesalers in the town, as well as to eager customers. Their jam-making reputation was even spreading to other towns in the West Riding, and absolute strangers began patronizing the little jam factory. As well as favourable word-of-mouth advertising, John also advertised his wares in, for those days, a 'Big Way' — he had an advertisement in *Christ Church (Woodhouse) Monthly Magazine, Huddersfield* (price 1*d*) in September 1900!

Expansion meant employing assistants to prepare the fruit. Jane was most particular who they were. Only the cleanest, most reputable of village women were invited to help. The workers' hair had to be neatly piled up into buns and tucked out of sight beneath clean mobcaps so that no stray hairs fell on to the fruit.

Eliza Pearson, one of the helpers in 'The Jam Factory'

Sober, ankle-length dresses were protected from stains by long pinafores, which were changed daily. Doubtless the assistants were staunch Methodists too, besides being deft at topping and tailing gooseberries and suchlike. They sat on small hard buffets encircling a huge earthenware bowl. Discarded stalks were emptied into an ashpit outside. The fruit was always cleaned with fresh leaves and never washed. 'You can't make good jam with wet fruit' was John's motto, and the strawberries had to be kept whole, not mushed up. Anybody could do it that slipshod way, but it didn't do for Taylor's.

Jane used to stand on the stone floor for hours, stirring the aromatic liquids with an enormous wooden spoon. No wonder she had bad legs in her later years. Not even she was permitted to clean the raspberries. That was John's province, and his alone. He staked his reputation on no grub, dead or alive, ever being found in his raspberry jams.

'The first time of cleaning,' he would murmur, meticulously scrutinizing each perfect berry, 'the first time, you nobbut disturb the grubs. The second time they come walking out.'

In those early days one could only get fruit when it was in season, and a nip of frost was usually in the air when marmalade-making time came round. The little jam factory must have been beautifully warm and inviting on a frosty winter morning, with golden marmalade bubbling in the pans and a bright coal fire burning in the grate.

But it must have been a hazardous business in the hot summertime keeping the wasps and flies at bay. Indeed, one village woman was employed for the sole purpose of standing guard with a rolled up newspaper to swat any winged interloper. Woe betide her if she drove it the wrong way and it accidentally fell into a cauldron of boiling jam!

The prices of those delicious home-made jams sound almost unbelievable today. A 2 lb jar for 1s, a 1 lb jar for 6d. And what luscious combinations of fruits there were! Strawberry and rhubarb, strawberry and gooseberry, blackberry and apple, raspberry and apple, red plum, greengage, Victoria plum – and not a preservative in sight. They were too appetizing in any case to remain for long in the pantry.

Another of Grandma's specialities was her delicious fancy jellies. Redcurrant and blackcurrant were her favourites, and it was said that the jellies were of a richness and flavour unsurpassed.

As the women worked they often sang hymns or recited, and there was never any lack of gossip. At mid-morning work stopped for mugs full of steaming cocoa, and pieces of Jane's home-made oatcakes, yet another of her specialities. Most days oatcakes could be seen drying over the wooden creel in the back kitchen behind the shop.

It truly was a family business. John's brother William, who owned the fields, stayed out there gathering the fruits most of the day, sitting down for sandwiches and a bottle of lemonade at midday and contemplating the sea of soft riches before him. Theoretically, anyway, that's what he was doing. But he confided to John that it was 'to keep out o' t'way of yon gossipy women'. Dinner over, his head would begin bobbing up over the hedges again. 'John!' he'd bellow, and another tray of ripe fruit would be placed on top of the wall for his brother to collect.

Jane's sister, Polly, helped cut circular jam covers from silk paper, and old Mrs Wakefield, who lived in one of the low deckers down the road, declared, 'It's a chance to earn mesen a bit o' spend.' The ladies had to bring their own buffets and scissors, and not forget their aprons.

John and Jane must have gazed out of their 'factory' window for many contented hours as they patiently stirred with those big wooden spoons that resembled ships' oars, counting the churches in the distance hundreds of times, never wearying of the view. Mirfield, Roberttown, Bradley – Grandad even had a big elderberry tree chopped down so as to give a clearer view. Of course, when it was time for the shop to open, Grandad had to leave the ladies to it.

It must have been a sad day for them all when, at the beginning of the First World War, John announced that there was no more sugar. The fruit juices began to run out of the factory door and customers were invited to bring dishes and take away as much fruit as they wished, free, rather than it be wasted. 'The Jam Factory', no larger than a decent-sized living room, was locked up.

Uncle William, the market gardener

Thereafter, until it was re-opened as a bakery later on, silence reigned in the outhouse which had once been the scene of so much activity, from which had emerged such a variety of tempting aromas. However, in the 1930s when my Dad took over the business, his brother Alfred having been killed in the First World War, appetizing aromas, though of a different kind, once again permeated the village through the open door. Home-made bread, jam and lemon cheese tarts, Eccles cakes, Madeira loaves . . . and another generation of Yorkshire children on their way to school stopped to sniff, Bisto Kid-like, with noses in the air.

CHAPTER THREE

AN OLD-TIME CHRISTMAS AT THE SHOP

Annie, John and Jane's first child, lived to be only eight, dying of diabetes. Even when only going for a short walk, a jug of water had to be carried for the thirsty little girl. Ever after, Annie's favourite dolls were encased in glass domes on the mantelpiece of the upstairs front room. Jane made them new clothes to wear each succeeding Christmas, and welcomed her widowed sister Elizabeth and her small daughter, also named Annie, when they visited at Christmas time. All the delights of the village shop gathered beneath one roof seemed like an Aladdin's cave to the poverty-stricken mother and daughter. Before they went to live permanently at the shop, Christmas was the highlight of the year for them. They set off to walk the few miles on Christmas Eve, but work had to be finished first. Elizabeth helped clean at a local doctor's, and had to give a final scouring to his front doorstep before she could think of her own pleasure. Little Annie was entrusted with wrapping up the gifts they had managed to scrape together, then put on her Sunday bonnet, cape and high-buttoned shoes to wait for the sound of her mother's key in the lock. Both were in a state of tremulous excitement. It was Christmas Eve at last.

What would Alfred and Joe, John and Jane's two young sons, have from Santa Claus? Perhaps they would allow Annie to play with their new toys for a while. Somehow she knew that Santa would not include her in his visit. Then she heard her mother's footsteps wearily plodding up the stone steps. After a hasty wash in the stone sink, and a change into her best black dress, shawl and boots, Elizabeth gave a final glance round the basement room to make sure all was in order. The door was locked, they set off a few paces, dashed back to retry the door, then they were really on their way. They walked to save tram fares.

John and Jane's first child, Annie

'You mustn't tell Uncle John or Aunt Jane that we walked', warned Annie's mother. 'Remember that we only do it for a bit of fresh air and the exercise.'

Of course, they wouldn't even have been able to afford the price of linen to make the daintily embroidered handkerchief gifts had they not watched where every penny went, and walked instead of riding whenever possible.

In those early years Joe and Alfred were models of decorum in the presence of the grown-ups. The children discussed their hopes for the coming night.

'I'd like some more tin soldiers,' declared Alfred, the eldest boy, while Joe would have been heartbroken had he not found a *Chatterbox Annual* in his stocking, and some watercolour paints, and a new brush and paper.

Being a girl, Annie was wiser. She knew that Santa had to budget. Her mother had told her so. She daren't hope for anything much. A packet of nuts and raisins, perhaps, an orange, and maybe a new penny. After all, it was the atmosphere that counted, the carol-singing and all that. Besides, she and her mother would have a warm bed for the night, and lovely meals the following day – what more could anyone expect or wish for?

The children had 'pobs' for supper, a concoction of warm milk with bread and treacle. Then three long woollen stockings were hung over the brass rail across the Yorkshire range. As Annie snuggled down beneath the blankets she could hear her cousins whispering to each other, then the plop of the gas jet as

The *Chatterbox Annual*, 1914. *Chatterbox* was
a weekly children's comic

they turned out the light. Before going to sleep, Annie made
sure that there was a good half of the bed for her mother. Then
it seemed no time at all, when, from out of a deep and dreamless
sleep, where not even Christmas morning mattered anymore, she
felt someone nudging her gently.

'Wake up, wake up, sleepyhead, or you won't have a bit of
Christmas.' It was her mother, and it was morning. Faintly at
first came the strains of the village brass band playing 'Christians
Awake, Salute The Happy Morn'. Annie could pick out the
deep, booming bass voice of Edward Langley, leader of the Band
of Hope and the local Methodist choir, accompanying the band.
How exciting it all was! *And* her stocking had been filled. The
orange deep in the toe, a little Japanese wooden doll, a selection
box – she'd seen some in the shop the last time they'd been to
tea – a diabolo game, a little storybook and other odds and ends.
She was ever so grateful to Santa Claus.

Alfred (left) and Joe Taylor, sons and heirs of Central Stores, Deighton

The grown-ups were soon busy about the house, laying fires in the upstairs front room in readiness for company in the afternoon, and a big crackling log and coal fire in the living-kitchen behind the shop. How the reflection of the flames gleamed on the dark brown Anaglypta on the walls, how cosy everything looked. Annie helped to prepare the Brussels sprouts, carrots and potatoes, then enjoyed helping to set the table, bringing out the clean starched tablecloth, and setting out the shining cutlery on it. Being staunch Methodists, no one expected, or even wanted, wine with the meal. Water, in clean tumblers, was perfect. So was the pork, and the apple and mustard sauce, and the sage and onion stuffing, then the big plum pudding and white sauce.

During the afternoon, before the last of the pale December sun – if there was any – disappeared, Aunt Polly and Uncle William would arrive. Mysterious bumps jutting out from beneath Aunt Polly's braided cape promised wonders in store. After the ladies had kissed beneath the solitary sprig of mistletoe – they weren't the kind to be promiscuous – outdoor clothes were ceremoniously folded on the quilt in the front bedroom. Hair was

Aunt Polly (centre) and friends

re-arranged, buns held together more firmly with little wavy grips, and snippets of news, not meant for gentlemen's ears, whispered before the family reunion in the sitting room above the shop.

John, conceding his strict teetotal rules for Christmas afternoon, handed diminutive glasses of home-made ginger wine round. Even the children, who sat with bated breath, hands folded in laps, awaiting the big moment when Polly remembered the parcels on the side table, had some. What would Polly's presents be? A monkey on a stick? Annie loved the way those monkeys leapt over the crossbar with a flick of the owner's wrist. Or maybe they contained a new ludo game, or a writing compendium? Perhaps a jar of pear drops, or motto lozenges? Wouldn't it be lovely if there was a French knitting set, thought Annie, so she could make little mats to stand vases on, and give them as birthday presents.

Present-exchanging over at last, everyone gathered round the piano to sing carols till teatime. Each had his or her favourite, and all clapped heartily after each solo. It was up to everyone to sing, and no one was allowed merely to sit about and expect to be entertained.

John's contribution never varied: 'Hail Smiling Morn'. Rarely was he as animated as on those occasions, except, perhaps, when he managed to cut a slice of bacon to the exact dimensions required by a customer. Guests waited expectantly for the inevitable, yearly tremor on the repeat line – 'Smiling morn, Smi-hi-ling Morn' – then the rush of sheer pleasure at the sound of his own voice, a good tenor, soaring to, 'That tips the hills with gold, that tips the hi-hills with gold.'

The ladies went downstairs to prepare high tea. What a spread! Cold pork, stuffing, cranberry sauce, brown and white bread on blue and white willow-pattern plates, trifles lost beneath lashings of fresh cream from the nearby farm, and decorated with hundreds and thousands (tiny dots of multi-coloured sweets), and even little silver balls, then the big iced Christmas cake and Stilton cheese, all 'washed down', as Polly described it, with lots of good strong tea.

There was plenty of hot water for washing up, with the fire in the Yorkshire range being stoked up all day. When everything was cleared away, the chenille cloth was spread evenly over the kitchen table and the aspidistra replaced in the centre next to the family Bible – it was games time.

This was Polly's opportunity to break loose. She was the wild one of the family, William's wife. Naturally though, in those days no woman was allowed to be really wild. But she did have a streak of devilment in her, which led to all manner of irresponsible, unladylike behaviour, such as swooping down on the poker, and rubbing it, soot and all, over her face to make herself look horribly like a witch, with John's best black velvet-collared coat thrown over her head. With hunched back she chased Annie, Joe and Alfred round and round the table till they were all dizzy, and begging for mercy and a game of charades. They were terrified, but wouldn't have missed the annual thrill for worlds. If Jane became too bustling and talkative (unseemly in a woman!), John could calm her at once with one look from his Methodist eyes. Not so with the irrepressible Polly. So if proceedings appeared to be getting at all unruly and out of hand, John decided it was time for a hot drink of milk or cocoa and a bit of quiet Bible reading.

Annie said that always, when grace was said in those far-off days, she prayed that all children, who, like her, had no father, may yet not be without an Uncle John and Aunt Jane on Christmas Day.

CHAPTER FOUR

A PRICELESS TREASURE

In the early years of Central Stores, before I was born, Grandma's sister, Elizabeth, and her daughter, Annie, were in residence for some years. Widowed, it was mutually beneficial both for Jane and Elizabeth. It suited Grandad too, to have a living-in helper. Annie won a scholarship to the new Girls' High School and homework was done on the kitchen table, with the continuous tinkle of the shop bell and customers banging in and out. No one lit fires in upstairs rooms in those days except on high days and holidays.

In the summer of 1912, Annie was sixteen, Alfred fourteen, and Joe nine. Jane decided that the children had worked hard and deserved a holiday.

'A breath of sea air will do them good,' she announced. She wasn't well enough to travel herself, and of course it would be quite unthinkable for John to leave the shop in someone else's care. He was one of those men who consider themselves indispensable. So it was arranged that Annie's mother, Elizabeth, would be the chaperone on the eagerly awaited jaunt to Colwyn Bay.

Jane wrote in her best copperplate handwriting to a boarding house named Pen-y-Mais. Schools were only closed for three weeks in summer then, and few could afford to go away at all. This excursion, however, was to be financed by Grandad, for the children did help a lot in the shop, weighing up flour and sugar, running errands without ever grumbling and cleaning shoes for the family. Even so, Elizabeth was conscious that it was her brother-in-law's money, and that they wouldn't have to be extravagant. It was agreed that another cousin – Cissie – would accompany them. Cissie was thirteen, and would be company for Annie.

The week prior to leaving saw much hustle and bustle in preparation for the big adventure. Large wicker baskets were packed with tea, sugar, butter and as many other provisions from the shop as possible, including a tin of salmon for the Sunday tea. They even took a joint of meat, but that had to be cooked first, as otherwise it would have been impossible to transport all that way on the train – raw, with all the blood running out. There was no such thing as frozen meat back in 1912, or if there was, it hadn't come the way of the ordinary family. Nor were there the plastic wrappers we have today. So the joint went in a heavy basin. Jane even made the gravy to save expense, and that travelled in one of her cough medicine bottles. The few clothes Annie had were parcelled up in brown paper and tied with string. Her only alternative footwear to the sensible brogues she wore every day was a pair of school pumps.

At 9.00 a.m. prompt, the dusty steam train puffed out of the station, bearing the excited group, with Joe and Alfred spick and span in second-best navy serge knickerbocker suits and straw sailor hats. Refreshment for the journey was a bag full of broken biscuits and bottles of home-made lemonade.

The long hot journey over, delighted yells of 'The sea! The sea!' erupted from the boys.

Pen-y-Mais was a clean, sober establishment of brown paintwork and sepia portraiture, a stag's head in the tiny hallway, and no other lodgers. Elizabeth prepared a tea of bread and jam, washed down with mugs of refreshing tea. How glorious it must have tasted, at journey's end, like finding gold at the end of the rainbow.

Then it was suggested that they might enjoy a little stroll to look at the sea. But there was to be no paddling or anything yet. They were all too tired, and besides, the tide was out. Elizabeth and the two girls sat down on a wooden bench to admire the view and take in deep breaths of sea air. But Joe and Alfred soon tired of that and became fidgety.

Annie, aged fifteen, and Cissie, aged twelve, 1910

'Can't we go a bit nearer, please, just for a little while?'

'Alright then, you two boys, you may walk on the promenade just a little way. But remember what I've said about paddling – not this evening.'

The trio on the hard wooden seat were dozing in the evening sunshine when Annie suddenly gave a cry of horror. Joe and Alfred were but specks on the far horizon, like tiny black silhouettes. Elizabeth hopped up and down in agitation, clutching her long skirt and setting off along the promenade in the direction of the errant figures.

'Hurry up Annie, Cissie, Aunt Jane will go mad if she finds out about this. Get to them – before they drown.'

When Annie, puffing and out of breath, reached her shamefaced cousins, Joe was 'crying buckets' and holding out his thick, home-knitted knee-length socks, dripping wet, in trembling hands.

Seaweed clung to them, and his boots were lined with the slimy stuff too. But they were safe from the 'raging sea' as Elizabeth chided them, though how could they disobey her, and in the very first hours at that. Already, she felt to have been proved inadequate to the trust placed upon her by her benefactors, Jane and John.

Alfred

'You naughty, naughty boys,' she admonished. 'You'll have caught your deaths of cold now. I wasn't reckoning on wearing mourning clothes again so soon.'

The disgruntled party hastened back to the boarding house, where, after cups of warm milk and a slice of currant teacake each (from Central Stores), the boys were sponged down with a jug of water from the large China bowl in the bedroom, dried, and put to bed in the small bedroom. Annie, Cissie and Elizabeth shared a huge brass bedstead in the next room. Joe and Alfred, in their striped flannelette nightshirts, had to be dosed with aconite before saying prayers. Then Elizabeth marched purposefully into the girls' room with spoon outstretched.

'But we haven't got wet!' they protested.

'Mebbe not,' sniffed Annie's mother, 'but you're having some just the same.'

It was a disappointing start to the long-awaited holiday. But the next day was better. They couldn't afford a lot of tram fares, so rode part of the way to Conway then walked the rest. They explored the castle and saw the smallest house in Great Britain. Then they bought halfpenny stamps, and wrote 'Having a lovely time – wish you were here' to those at home at the shop on the backs of postcards.

On the promenade were pierrots in pale grey costumes, with big fluffy pompoms on their conical hats. Joe and Alfred parted with 2d for a seat on a mat to watch the concert, while the others, less reckless with their money, decided against paying for deck chairs and stood at the back, dodging the collecting tin when it came round.

There was one treat each day. A cream bun to 'finish off' with at tea-time. What debates took place outside the little confectioner's window, as the eager children pressed their noses against the pane, wondering which cream-filled delight to choose! Joe was always faithful to a 'team horn' – his childlike way of pronouncing cream horn – and staunchly refused to be diverted from his favourite throughout the week. Although 'Uncle John' had provided money for this daily treat, nevertheless, if they enjoyed hard-boiled eggs and lettuce first, there was no stewed fruit and custard as well. Or if they chose fruit, there was no boiled ham. One had to be forsaken. They were fortunate to be having a holiday as it was, without being greedy. In any case, that kind of tea was for Sundays only at the shop. Usually it was simply chunky slices of bread and jam – their own delicious, can't-have-enough-of-it, home-made jam.

One day the holiday-makers went to Llandudno, where another aunt and her daughters Adelaide and Charlotte were staying. They wanted to go up to the Great Orme, but could only manage to take two of the young visitors with them. Six was too many to be responsible for. Getting prematurely wet and seaweeded up was one thing, but toppling over the Great Orme was quite another, so it was decided that Annie and Alfred were the most suitable candidates. Cissie may be a hazard, being something of a tomboy, and Joe was too young.

Thus it was arranged, much to Joe's discontent. He and Cissie were relegated to being taken by the ladies to Happy Valley. Pretty, but not adventurous whatsoever. Wildly disappointed, Joe muttered 'not Happy Valley – Miserable Valley', and called it that to the end of his days.

On the whole, however, all thoroughly enjoyed their holiday. The sun shone, the sky was perennially blue, and best of all, there were cream buns for tea every single day. After the shopping was finished in the mornings, there was the swing in the back garden of Pen-y-Mais, and a little black kitten called Nigger who lived there. How they adored Nigger, who kept sidling up to the visitors to be nursed or played with. Occasionally they splashed out on a penny magazine or comic, handing it round between them. And not every day, but sometimes, the children bought a halfpenny ice-cream cornet each, trying to lick it quickly before the hot sun melted it away.

On the Friday before they were to return to the shop on the following day, the children held a conference on the seashore. They had already bought gifts for friends and relations at home, all inscribed with 'A Present From Colwyn Bay', but it was resolved that as they had had such a wonderful holiday, they must buy something for 'Aunt Elizabeth' for looking after them. But what? Furthermore, where was the money to come from? Alfred, Joe, Cissie and Annie turned out their pockets and totted up the pathetic remains of their spending money. Cissie managed 1½d, and Annie and Alfred forked out 2d each. Joe stood silent, straw hat pushed to the back of his sunbleached hair, hands thrust deep into his knickerbocker pockets, contemplating something far out to sea.

'Come on now, Joe,' ordered big brother Alfred.

'I 'aven't got anyfing left,' mumbled Joe.

Alfred tapped his brother's pocket.

'You've a halfpenny left, you know you have.'

So Joe, reluctantly, had to hand over the coin to the 'Presentation Fund'. But they still had to find something suitable. They searched and searched and held innumerable debates, while Aunt Elizabeth crocheted in the sun. Then they spied a little hardware shop. In the window was a small wooden implement with a scrap of emery paper stuck on it. The price decided them. It was exactly 6d.

'Just the thing!' all agreed, and jostled their way into the dark little shop, handing over their accumulated coinage.

Cissie, who, although a tomboy, had a feeling for the niceties of life, announced, 'We will have to have a proper presentation and speech.'

The ceremony was to take place after the teatime cream buns had been devoured. The honour of handing over the brown paper gift was to go to the youngest, Joe, in part to vindicate himself from the near disastrous start to the week. Alfred and Cissie deliberated long over the wording of the speech, before the latter stood to attention in that drab little boarding house. Haltingly, but charmingly, the little speech was delivered, then Joe stepped forward and handed over the parcel to Aunt Elizabeth. She nearly cried, but didn't want to risk ruining her

Cousin Annie with Alfred (standing), Joe
and Uncle George at the back of the shop

best lace-edged handkerchief. All was forgiven and almost
forgotten, and the wicker baskets packed much lighter than
when they had set forth.

Joe's Aunt Elizabeth, he told me years afterwards, kept the
queer little emery-backed object as long as she lived.

'It was never a right lot of use,' she admitted, 'but, oh, what a
priceless treasure!'

CHAPTER FIVE

THE FIRST WORLD WAR – THE WIND OF FATE

When Alfred left Huddersfield Boys' College it was decided he would become an apprentice grocer at a tiptop shop in the town. His father wanted him to learn the trade properly. He was a 'grand lad', always cheerful, bright and intelligent. Keenly interested in photography as a hobby, he had already made a number of postcards of local scenes, and was selling them in the shop. He kept his huge camera and a box of glass slides in the attic.

Then came the First World War, and Alfred, like so many others, put on a soldier's uniform. He was stationed at Rugeley Camp in Staffordshire, and Joe was now attending the college. Younger brother Joe had high hopes of becoming either a scientist or chemist, after passing the Cambridge Junior examination with flying colours.

Their mother Jane was becoming increasingly crippled with rheumatism, so a local woman, Mrs Hudson, came in daily to 'fettle round' for her. She was known as the 'Queen of the Black-lead Brushes' by some!

One day the postman brought word that Alfred was seriously ill with spotted fever. It was a bitterly cold January, and Jane

Young Alfred, dressed for an occasion

wasn't fit to travel, so John went by train alone. When he reached his son's bedside, Alfred had packets of cigarettes on the bed that other young soldiers had given to him. He was, he told his father, practising 'being a grocer' for when the war was over and he came home.

'Have you any message, Alfred?' asked his distraught father.

'Love to mother – and tell Joe to be a good boy.'

A few days later Jane and John were ill in bed with influenza, with Joe and Annie doing their homework in the kitchen, and Mrs Hudson 'looking on' for 'Mr and Mrs Taylor'. The shop door bell tinkled. A GPO boy handed a telegram to Mrs Hudson. Her hand shook as she returned to the kitchen.

'It's come,' she announced to Annie and Joe. Both began to weep, and Punch sidled up to them, resting his head first on one of their knees then the other, as though to say, '*I'm* still here, do cheer up.'

On the day of the funeral the body of nineteen-year-old Alfred Castle Taylor was taken straight to the churchyard, it being deemed too infectious to be brought into the house. The funeral tea was catered for by the shop, the table being fully extended and set out before the sad entourage left for the chapel. Sadly, the mourners bowed their heads as the son and heir to Central Stores was lowered gently into the deep grave, leaving plenty of room for when John and Jane, and, many years later, Joe followed.

Joe was saddened by more than the loss of a beloved brother. For now the mantle of grocer, and helping his parents, fell upon him. He hadn't wanted to become a grocer – Alfred had. His dreams of becoming a scientist or chemist or something in that line vanished as inevitably as the coffin was lost to sight beneath the soil forever. Joe now had to be groomed for the shop, after he left the boys' college. In the years immediately after the First World War, before the era of most commodities being pre-packaged, there was much more scope for the Weights and Measures Man to swoop and make a kill. John lived in dread of him. Meticulous as he was about fairness, he was accountable even for the others who helped 'weigh up' in the shop. Almost everything arrived loose, and it was then up to the shopkeeper to make sure they were weighed exactly right, or he could face a fine. Worse, he could lose his good name.

There was no such thing as ready-washed currants, raisins and sultanas. John had a riddle – a large object with fine mesh surrounded by wood to hold the dried fruits in. When they had been thoroughly cleaned and the stalks nipped off, the fruits were pushed round and round in the riddle before the kitchen fire to dry. Candied peel came in thick, exotic-looking half-moon shapes, encrusted with sticky sugar, and customers had to dice it into small cubes themselves at home. A popular brand of tea was Mazawatee. It arrived at the shop in big drums with pictures of Chinese mandarins adorning the exterior, as did the loose coffee.

Alfred, aged eighteen, August 1917

Joe, aged sixteen, *c.* 1919

Vinegar was measured into bottles from a big wooden barrel with a tap at the side. It never turned off completely, and at that spot on the shop floor there was always a vague vinegary smell. An attached funnel dispensed the vinegar into the customers' bottles. Treacle was kept in a barrel too, and what a sticky operation it used to be opening up the kegs and waiting for the syrup to ooze slowly into the waiting jar. In order to calculate the amount, and therefore price, of the treacle the trick was to weigh the customer's container first, then again with the treacle inside. In later years, when Mother, no mathematician, arrived on the scene, she was always foxed by the complicated procedure. She invariably forgot to weigh the container initially, so no one ever knew how to charge for treacle weighed out by her.

Customers would never buy cheese without sampling a piece first. Stilton was only bought in for the Christmas trade, unless by special request of some of the nobler customers, such as the local preacher or the doctor's wife. Cheese was wrapped in thick white 'cap' paper.

Friday was the fashionable day for edging doorsteps with donkey stone – each had a donkey imprint which wore away through use – and for washing bedroom windows as well. Fel's naphtha soap was excellent for washing dirty overalls , and the Fairy soap took up a lot of space beneath the counter. The shop sold lots of White Windsor and bright-red carbolic, and popular for scrubbing grime out were tins of soft soap called Sheep Dip, which had a jelly-like consistency. Cherry Blossom boot polish was a favourite, though why anything so black or deep brown could be likened to pink blossom I never could fathom. Lots of wooden gipsy clothes pegs were sold on Monday mornings. Everything that had been washed by Monday evening was stiff and starchy: shirts, blouses, dressing table sets, runners for sideboards, and those bits of material that fussy women used to drape over their couches, presumably to soak up mens' hair grease.

Once a piece of furniture was acquired in those days, it was expected to last a lifetime, and must be looked after. At one time a soap firm used to give a free towel in exchange for every twelve soap wrappers collected. One customer never had to buy a towel all through her married life.

For many years bacon was sliced by hand – John's – with a sharp black-handled knife specially kept for the job. It was not until Joe took over most of the running of the shop that a bacon machine was installed. Customers watched intently as Grandad made tentative touches at the side of the bacon. 'Here?' 'A bit thicker?' 'Yes, exactly right.' The great advantage of cutting it by hand was that customers could see what thickness it was, and hadn't to remember what number setting on a machine it was they wanted. John used to boil hams in 'The Jam Factory', and sold them at 6d a quarter. The fame of that ham went to one end of the village and back, and to a few more surrounding ones besides. It was said to be absolutely delicious, especially with a few big pickles, and it certainly had a far more distinctive flavour than its counterparts do today.

Eggs had no specially shaped containers. Customers simply had to be extra careful when carrying them. Sometimes they brought a white basin or wicker basket to transport them home in. Otherwise, John or Jane counted them carefully into a white paper bag with the warning 'Now be careful how you go' or 'Watch out for any banana skins Mrs So and So.'

John and Jane, with Punch the dog

CHAPTER SIX

HILDA – A TWENTIES' FLAPPER

Hilda, the girl who Joe was eventually to marry and bring to the shop as the new Mrs Taylor, was a very different kettle of fish to Jane. Born in Boroughbridge in January 1901, six hours after Queen Victoria died – the quickest reincarnation of all time one would think, the way she never let people forget the coincidence – her mother instilled it into her that she, Hilda, had been born to fill the gap left by the queen. The Boroughbridge village constable's daughter probably never imagined she would end up in a village shop. She always imagined, especially with her dark good looks, that she was destined for great things.

In the twenties she was a typical flapper. She was bright, vivacious and giddy as a kipper, and as crazy about boys as they were mad about her, though she never went dancing until she was married and in her thirties. Joe didn't dance, and Hilda's parents thought dancing 'only for sluts'. And as for girls who wore lipstick! Well, they were bound to 'go the wrong way'. So any boyfriends were village worthies, or, when the family moved to the West Riding from Boroughbridge, young men she

Hilda Haigh – an early photograph

encountered either on her way to work in a millinery and gown
shop or at chapel.

Hilda – later to become my Mother – recalls working in the
Emporium, as some of those establishments were grandly named,
helping ladies choose dresses to flatten their bosoms and to
match their eyes. It was a job where not too much concentration
was required, and where a pleasant, helpful manner was more
important than being a mathematical genius. She remembers the
time when one well-to-do lady of the town went in for a yard of
elastic. There wasn't much left on the roll, but it hardly seemed
worthwhile opening a new one. A bit flustered, Hilda
absentmindedly stretched what there was, pulling it to try and fit
the yard mark on the edge of the counter! The customer
imperiously signalled for the manageress.

'Tut, tut, tut, young lady, that will never do!' she admonished
Hilda, when told of her misdeed.

'I could cheerfully have strangled both of them with the
damned elastic,' she remembered. After all, she was born for
better things than measuring out elastic for middle-aged ladies'
knickers.

Hilda much preferred titivating hats to anything else; she could
daydream then. There were plenty of idle moments on Mondays

when the majority of women were slaving over peggy tubs and mangles. Then Hilda and the other young assistants could chat about the past weekend and the boy of the moment, at the same time sipping their morning coffee and savouring freshly-baked French buns with lovely sticky white icing from Whiteley's, the confectioner's in the arcade.

From the workroom window upstairs, Hilda had a bird's-eye view of the young men in the office windows opposite. One who especially appealed to her she privately nicknamed Blue Eyes. Sometimes, as though conscious of the inquisitive lively hazel eyes watching him from Flack's Emporium across the way, he raised his dark, well-shaped head. Sometimes he smiled shyly. As time went by, the intimacies of the window romance became more daring. One lazy, hot summer afternoon Blue Eyes' behaviour became quite deliciously outrageous. One dares more, perhaps, in summer sunshine than in the dull, monotonous grey of winter. Anyhow, Miss Fletcher who was first sales assistant and no nonsense, was out at lunch at the Princess Café, a cosy little place beneath the cinema. Blue Eyes took his opportunity. He actually began to blow kisses across to Hilda. She was no good for the rest of the day, except for fits of uncontrollable giggles with the others.

In the twenties, when girls were invited to the pictures – the Empire, the Princess, or perhaps the Tudor – they were escorted by 'a young man'. There was nothing so common as what is nowadays termed a date, or worse, a bloke, or chap. Closing time at the Emporium on Saturday evenings was eight o'clock, so visits to the cinema were preferred on Wednesday evenings, half-day closing. What high hopes there were in the last few minutes before closing time! Hilda kept nipping into the assistants' rest room to attend to her coiffeur if she was going out straight from work. This consisted of thrusting a pair of iron curling tongs into the flames of the gas fire, and crimping her jet-black hair into waves, a hazardous operation as, more often than not, with the hot tongs twisted and enmeshed in her hair, she began to daydream about Blue Eyes or her other admirers, but being brought quickly down to earth by the pungent smell of sizzling hair.

On Saturday nights and other special occasions Hilda sported 'side bits', two large waves pulled forwards to curve enticingly

Hilda and Joe on a trip with friend, Nellie Gibson (right)

over each cheekbone. A couple of kiss curls on her forehead completed the flapper hairstyle. Despite her parents' ban on make-up, she had a pot of Pond's vanishing cream, and a little tin of powder rouge which she kept hidden in a drawer at work and which she applied discreetly, remembering to rub it off before entering the house. A daring touch was the smear of Vaseline on her already long, lustrous black eyelashes. She never wore any lipstick, for even Hilda thought that that would be going a bit too far, and a bit common. Nevertheless, prior to meeting the young man of the moment, she bit her lips viciously before emerging from the Emporium, to encourage them to appear red and inviting. Her nails were buffed with pink rouge from a tin. Hilda changed her black dress for a white crêpe de Chine blouse and low-waisted navy skirt, plus a provocative little cloche hat if a young man was calling for her. She adored her blouse with a fringe of heavy silk tassels hanging from the shoulders, and thought she really looked the bee's knees. Low-heeled shoes with straps completed her ensemble, with a Dolly Varden bag to carry her handkerchief and purse.

Occasionally, because of her exceptional good looks, Hilda was asked to wear a fox fur from the shop at weekends, providing she gave an undertaking to keep it clean and to tell as many people as possible where they could purchase a similar beautiful object.

Young men never forgot to raise their trilby or bowler on meeting the lady of their choice. Indeed, if they'd been properly brought up, they tilted their hat to any lady, young or old, or ugly. They also believed in dressing smartly when a young lady did them the honour of going out with them, right down to kid gloves and impeccable stiff white collar, and maybe even the loan of father's albert, suspended across a youthful waist.

It was extra special to be escorted to the Theatre Royal. One exceedingly tall and gangling young man, a millowner's son from Dewsbury, was absolutely *loopy* about Hilda. He arranged to take her to 'The Royal' one Saturday evening, to the second performance. As soon as they met he pressed an enormous box of chocolates into her arms. But for some reason, maybe the manner in which his plus fours hung around his elongated legs, or the too-big peak on his checked cap (Hilda preferred those romantic-looking fluffy velour trilbies; she could run her fingers over the fluff flirtatiously), she suddenly knew that she couldn't possibly spend the whole evening in his company, even at 'The Royal'. She instinctively knew that he would end up being more fitted for golf than romance. Yet, kind at heart and hating to hurt anyone, she had a brainwave.

'Poor dear mamma has sent a message that she has a most awful headache and a terrible bilious round. How kind you are, but I can't possibly accept the chocolates now, when I have to dash home.'

Young men in those days, if they were well brought up especially, seemed to wear their hearts on their sleeves much more than they do today. It felt absolutely criminal for Hilda to have to disappoint him. Besides, the millowner's son was so 'gone' on Hilda that the refusal caused him to blush crimson, which didn't at all suit the orangey checks of his plus fours. All the tragedy of the ages seemed mirrored in his eyes.

In youthful enthusiasm, though near to tears, he gushed, 'But I really must insist that you accept them, my dear. I bought them

Joe, Hilda and friends, *c.* 1920

specially for you. And please give your dear mamma one when she recovers.'

They walked together in embarrassed silence to the tram stage. The last Hilda ever saw of him was his moonstruck gaze, dejected plus fours, and air of sheer despondency as he waved to her while she rattled out of sight, and out of his life, on the tramcar.

On Sunday evening Hilda took her usual place in the choir at chapel. She noticed a handsome young man staring at her from the back pew. He began to smile sheepishly whenever he caught her laughing eyes, then dawdled about in the tree-lined chapel walk after the service.

'Excuse me miss – er –,' murmured Joe, the grocer's son from Central Stores.

'Haigh. Hilda Margaret,' replied the girl of his dreams.

'Would you mind if I saw you home?' asked Joe.

It wasn't long before Joe had an audition to be in the choir too. The choirmaster was a fastidious little tenor who did his

Joe and Hilda in 1923, the year they were married

best to use all the correct pronunciations, as he held such an important position, but somehow the words always came out wrong, except when he was singing. Hilda could barely contain her giggles when he approached her after chapel one warm summer evening. Dashing towards her with his notepad, pencil poised in mid-air in affected manner, he asked in his ridiculously falsetto voice, 'Now Miss Haigh, you will do us the honour of accompanying the rest of us on the chara trip I presume – and you too, Mr Taylor?'

It wasn't long before the young man from Central Stores who had taken a fancy to Hilda from the back pew in chapel bought her a sparkling engagement ring. It cost £13, and the happy couple were presented with a butter knife as a gift from the jeweller. In tremulous excitement Hilda flashed her latest acquisition before the astonished eyes of Miss Fletcher on the following Monday morning. Without so much as lifting her eyes from stitching on braid and beads to a customer's dress, she sniffed loudly and muttered, 'I have my doubts about you, Miss Haigh. I think it's just the ring you're going for.'

CHAPTER SEVEN

WEDDING BELLS

The marriage of Hilda and Joe was to prove much stormier than the staunch, loyal and true one of John and Jane. On the latter's silver wedding anniversary the village poet presented them with an apt tribute in verse. Penned in broad Yorkshire, this is how it goes:

DARBY TO JOAN

Ay does ta remember owd lass when we wed?
It's twenty-five year sin today –
When I – well I promised to love thee, tha knows,
An' thee – well tha said tha'd obey.
Han we kept to us word? Well, i' th' main happen, yuss.
We'n had ups an daans net a few –
But we've both pull'd together, an i' th'words o' th'owd song,
Tha's allus been 'loving an' true'.
We've loved an' we've lost, but we've nivver lost faith
In Him that is moor than a friend,
He knows what's best for us – we see it all naah,
Soa we'll trust Him reight on to Life's end.
A chap said t'other day, 'Why John tha looks well
After twenty-five year wear an' tare,
But he worn't wed, an' of course cudn't see
'At o'd thee all me troubles to share.
I know I've my faults, ther's noan on us baat,
Tha has some thisen, tha'll agree,
But tha's o'erlooked my failings, aye monny a time,
An' I've tried to do th' same lass by thee.

Joe and Hilda during their courting days

I call thee 'owd lass' but we arrent owd yet,
We're just in us prime, thee an' me.
Starting on a new lease o' twenty-five year –
For we hoap th' Golden Wedding ta see.
An' when that day comes, in this place we both love,
May us friends rally raand – as toneet –
That is if God wills – but if some are not here,
Then we hope all in Heaven to meet.

Obey? Hilda had no intention of obeying, husband or anyone. She enjoyed, however, the weeks preceding the wedding that would culminate in her joining Jane and John at Central Stores. Annie and her mother by that time had moved out, Annie to become a teacher, and they had found a tiny rented house of their own. But the reality of having to share accommodation with her in-laws had never really crossed Hilda's girlish, romantic mind.

About a month before the great day, 19 September 1923, she went by tramcar into town to choose her wedding dress. She decided on white crêpe de Chine, which revealed her ankles when worn. She bought white artificial silk stockings and a pair of white shoes, which were low, with a Cuban heel, straps and buttoned. She thought she was being madly extravagant buying the veil, which was to be worn low on the brow. It cost all of £3, but was beautifully decorated with orange blossom. Huge lilies were ordered for the bouquet, thus keeping the virginal white theme throughout the whole ensemble. Perhaps lilies were the wrong choice; aren't they supposed to be unlucky for weddings?

Hilda's sisters, Ella and Winnie, were to be bridesmaids, and Joe's cousin, Annie. Winnie, then about fourteen, wore black stockings, a white low-waisted dress and a very large cape collar, as well as a single string of artificial pearls (one could get them from Woolworths for 6d then, I think), white gloves and a big black Panama hat. Ella went shopping and chose a wide-brimmed velour hat with a broad ribbon band. But she insisted that she wasn't going to have a plain white dress. She chose an eye-catching one with a neckline decorated with rows of coloured braids, and zigzag stripes edging the draped collar. There were also three bands of braid on the hemline of the ankle-length skirt. Doubtless Ella, always a dominant, forceful character, hoped she'd stand out more than the bride wearing that bobby-dazzler. Deep red carnations were ordered for all three bridesmaids to carry in their white-gloved hands, another well-known bad luck combination for weddings. White and red, which should never, ever, be combined if disaster is not to be courted. Of course, they didn't know anything about such folklore.

There were no worries about lipstick shades. None of the Haigh girls would have, at that time, sullied their mouths with it – too common for words! But plenty of lip-biting went on beforehand, as well as discreet dabs of Pond's, with perhaps a puff of palest powder to remove the shine from their noses and foreheads. They looked, and no doubt were, three spotless virgins.

Hilda's home had no bathroom before her marriage. There was only a big zinc bath in the cellar. Bathrooms in suburbia were rare in the 1920s.

'Besides gaining a husband, I'll be gaining a bathroom as well!' Hilda had boasted to her unmarried sisters.

'Don't forget what else you'll have thrown into the bargain – your husband's mother and father,' snapped back Ella.

The wedding was fixed for early in the morning, so the lack of a proper bathroom posed a bit of a problem for Hilda, as no bride-to-be wants to go to her new husband unbathed.

'We can't do with you having a bath in front of the fire on your wedding morning,' declared Mrs Haigh. 'Who knows who may be popping in and out with good wishes, and to have a last look at you.'

'To say nothing of the vicar dropping in to check the hymn numbers,' laughed Ella.

The predicament solved a problem for a neighbour. What to give Hilda for a present? The neighbour had gone up in the world, and now boasted a proper bathroom in her house. She offered the use of it to Hilda for however long she wished to use it. Hilda remembers the luxury of being completely submerged with lovely hot soapy water, instead of the top bits roasting by the fire and a cold draught at the back should any of the Haigh family come in or out during her ablutions. As an additional gift the neighbour had put out a big tin of Ashes of Roses talcum powder and a couple of thick Turkish towels to dry the bride on. When she emerged, Hilda felt to be a fit consort for a king, let alone a village grocer.

Cousin Annie, who became a school-mistress, in the 1920s

Of course, permission to wed at all, even at twenty-three, had first to be granted.

'You know quite well about my bilious rounds and bad legs Hilda,' her mother had wept, when the engagement had first been mooted. 'You know I rely on you to go over the coconut matting on Thursdays. You can't expect me to get down on the floor with a brush and shovel, not at my age, and in my condition.'

Such was parental obedience then that although it was on the tip of Hilda's tongue to ask, 'What about the others? What about Ella or Winnie?', she refrained. So a verbal contract was drawn up whereby the new Mrs Taylor would return to her maiden home every Thursday to go over the coconut matting and clean the doorsteps, and do any other job that her mother required.

'Girls don't think about their old parents nowadays' was the reply to Hilda's declaration of love for the grocer's son, a declaration that necessitated her father dashing for the smelling salts to bring round her mother, who was clutching her ample bosom and vowing that 'the Lord had come for her'.

Even the night before her wedding, Hilda was severely rebuked by her scandalized mamma because she didn't arrive home until 10 p.m.

'The neighbours will think you're a right bad lot coming in at this unearthly hour,' she was reprimanded. However, there was still time for the errant bride-to-be to wash her hair with Amami shampoo for brunettes, and to dry it before the blazing coal fire, while her mother railed on about the sins of staying out late.

There wasn't the mass exodus to hairdressers then, even for a special occasion such as a wedding. Guests simply washed their hair in a bowl at home, then rolled it up into the usual bun at the back. Cleanliness, not sophistication, was the keyword of the middle-class Yorkshirewoman.

Hilda couldn't see the sense of having yards of hair flowing down her back, only to have to roll it up into those hideous buns so that it appeared almost shorter than an Eton crop. It must have taken ages to dry without the aid of a hairdryer. No wonder many girls set aside a whole evening to wash their hair. Then there was the hundred strokes of the brush nightly that some swore by, and rubbing Harlene into the scalp to encourage better growth and healthier hair. The bride-to-be's mother was a firm believer in 'plenty of dumplings to stick to the ribs' for first-class health, both of body and hair. Hair was kept in tiptop condition by frequent singeings too.

Hilda had had her hair cut in the new bobbed style, so she only had to frizz it up a bit after getting into her wedding dress. She had to be extra careful with it that morning, as she didn't want it to go up in flames or to turn out too frizzy.

It was a formal wedding. John, the groom's father, stylish in tall black silk hat, stiff white collar with wings, watch chain and albert across his waistcoat, looked more like a lawyer than a village grocer on the wedding photograph. All the lady guests wore hats of mammoth proportions, some garlanded with what appeared to be complete gardens. The gentlemen had alberts draped across their middles – even the quite young ones. One relation, Blanche, wore a white tulle concoction of a hat with an outsize red rose coquettishly centred on the drooping brim.

Major Bell, who was at that time keen on Ella, never managed to make much headway in his manoeuvres, either in the chase or in the churchyard wedding grouping. He was so short that a buffet had to be brought for him to stand on. All the Sunday school chairs had been brought out for the guests to sit on. After all, it took a long time to be photographed, with the photographer having to disappear beneath the black camera cover every so often, then darting out again if someone blinked or moved.

Even though Hilda and Joe's wedding day turned out to be one of those halcyon Indian summer ones, with blue skies and sunshine, and gold and brown leaves crackling underfoot, a few elderly relatives didn't miss the opportunity of hanging their prized fox furs round their scrubbed necks.

Not many of the twenty-three or so assembled people actually smiled for the photograph. Most looked as though they had just witnessed a funeral. Maybe John and Jane did spare a thought for the grave of their eldest son, Alfred, lying in the cold earth not far away, and secretly wondered how the attractive, vivacious-looking girl would settle down to living at the shop. Jane, in anticipation of a new helper, had already – most unwisely as it turned out – given notice to her 'daily'. With both Jane and Hilda in residence beneath the same roof, Hilda would have to knuckle under or there were sure to be some personality clashes and flare-ups.

At the reception in the Sunday school, Hilda's brothers George, Alec and Willie were resplendent in their brand-new billycocks and trilbies, billycock being the name for a bowler hat. During the meal the hats were hung on pegs which lined the walls. Hilda's mother was in a state of acute apprehension, elegant in a taffeta floor-length gown with a huge velvet hat shading her handsome features.

They all ate boiled ham fresh from Central Stores, assorted pickles and jars of red cabbage which were placed at intervals down the long tables. Then there were jellies and blancmanges, and iced buns with cherries on top. The impressive wedding cake was at the top of the table in front of the bride and her groom, and had been sent down from the shop. Tea was poured from two big urns at either end of the white, starchy tables by volunteers from the Ladies' Tuesday Bright Hour. They all wore black artificial silk dresses and little white aprons, and laughed a lot.

After the wedding breakfast a friend who actually owned a car – an Austin 7 – ran the newlyweds back to the shop so that Hilda could change into her going-away outfit, a navy blue serge costume, ankle length, with a white artificial silk blouse and lots of fancy frills down the front and little pearl buttons. There was also a beautiful new fox fur, complete with proper fox face, which rested on her chest and fastened with a silky chain. The Emporium had lent it to her for the honeymoon, with the proviso that she must remember to say where it had originated from. The rest of her ensemble was a large-brimmed velvet hat and new kid gloves. A serviceable brown suitcase carried the rest of the trousseau.

Then the happy pair, the future owners of Central Stores, were whisked away by steam train to Whitby. There they billed and cooed in a tiny fisherman's cottage down by the harbour. They had a tiny attic bedroom with a sloping roof, on which they were to suffer many a cracked head. There was also a great deal of clomping backwards and forwards throughout the night as burly fishermen passed by outside, singing, drinking and uttering oaths. Fish and chips, eaten from newspapers, was their first supper together as Mr and Mrs Taylor.

Hilda and Joe had bought a Brownie box camera and had a wonderful time, especially as they both loved music and singing, listening to the songs of the twenties at shows, and their very favourite, 'Wedding Bells will Ring so Merrily'. Those light-hearted lovers were an endearing mixture of romance, daftness and sheer *joie de vivre*, epitomized by energetic renderings of another then well-known hit:

> In the twi-twi-twilight,
> Out in the beautiful twilight,
> They all go out for a walk, walk, walk,
> A quiet old spoon and a talk, talk, talk.
> That's the time they long for, just before the night,
> And many a grand little wedding is planned
> In the twi-twi-light.

After the honeymoon, a new and boisterous period was to begin at Central Stores, so different from the staid, orderly rule of John and Jane.

CHAPTER EIGHT

FIRST A BOY, AND THEN A GIRL

Hilda, her new in-laws soon discovered, had an amazing aptitude for delegating work to others that she did not enjoy herself. In the first few weeks she sincerely meant well and wanted to help. She offered to scrub the shop floor on her first Wednesday half-day closing to create a good impression.

'It will save you getting down on your knees, as they are a bit rheumaticky,' she said to Jane.

When Hilda had finished, the floor was spotless. But in her enthusiasm she had accidentally knocked over a huge bottle of ammonia. It had swamped the floorboards, and the fumes had enveloped everything. Hilda swept up the glass and deposited it in the dustbin, and thought no more about the incident. Until next day, when, a few hours after opening time, customers kept returning. There was a steady stream of anxious faces and furrowed brows, bringing back butter and other commodities.

'We're very sorry – we've never had to complain before. But there's a queer taste – we can't understand it.'

The spilt ammonia had tainted everything in the shop.

'Perhaps it wasn't such a good idea to sack Mrs Hudson after all,' commented John, with a doubtful glance at Hilda.

'No, perhaps it wasn't,' flashed back his daughter-in-law. 'I didn't marry your son just to come here and be a skivvy!'

Another day she thought it would be a pleasant enough task putting a freshly-baked batch of ginger buns on display on top of the counter. They had been brought in from the bakehouse, which the old 'Jam Factory' had been turned into. But unfortunately for Hilda, they had been balanced precariously on one end of a flour bin. When a particularly charming commercial traveller appeared in the shop doorway Hilda tipped the whole lot into the open flour bin in her confusion.

Hilda and Philip,
c. 1927

There was an ideal solution for Hilda to get away from living with her in-laws – having a family of her own. A private nurse attended Hilda as she awaited the birth of her first child in the back bedroom over the shop. She personally supervised and cooked her patient's meals, and both she and Dr Copeland, who delivered her son on 19 October 1925, pronounced Mother a perfect patient. It was to her advantage to do exactly as she was told, so for once she did. Philip was the chosen name, with Gordon as an additional one to please Dr Gordon Copeland.

On 10 April 1927 I put in an appearance, also in the bedroom over the shop. But this time the private nurse was called to an emergency not long after I was born, so Hilda wasn't mollycoddled for long. Neither was I. I was turned over to the somewhat rough and ready care of Mrs Hudson, while Mother fully recuperated from her exertions.

Mrs Hudson, wholesome with workworn hands and roughened elbows, was at least eminently reliable. If lacking the airs and graces of the private nurse, and more used to black-leading the Yorkshire range than bathing a newly born baby, I still recall the experience as entirely delightful. Being held across Mrs Hudson's knees was a bit like I should imagine it felt like to be safe in the arms of Jesus. At bathtime the bathroom was a fog of steam, with fleeting glimpses of Mrs Hudson's red face, if I happened to be lying on my back. The whole room was aromatic with clouds of lavender talcum powder, or Cusson's soap, or Johnson's baby powder. There was never any occasion to stint oneself. 'There's plenty more in the shop' was mother's

Philip and Hazel, *c.* 1929

Hilda with friends, including Winnie
Halstead and Ella Lunn (in the sidecar),
c. 1926. Philip is in the front

motto. Those liberal bathtimes must have made me quite
impervious to the notion that things had to be paid for. Because
one could walk into the shop and lay hands on whatever was
required, the feeling that they had to be paid for somehow didn't
apply to us.

In a glow of warmth and contentment I was wrapped in a
shawl and carried downstairs to the living-kitchen where my
flannelette nightie was warming over the big brass fireguard. This
was not a tiny affair that merely covered the aperture of the fire
itself, but one that stood majestically all the way round the range.

Some while after my birth we left the shop to live in a private
house not far away, and Dad went to work there daily. Every
Monday our other Grandad, the tall lanky one who always wore
a black suit and bowler hat, and who had been a policeman in
his younger days, came to play with Philip and me. On fine
afternoons at haymaking time he took us out to the field at the
back of our house, and made an aeroplane. Concorde wouldn't

have stood a chance against those creations. A big heap of hay was the aeroplane's nose, and a scooped out hollow formed the cockpit where Grandad, in black suit liberally streaked with golden hay, sat and piloted. Two more hay hollows behind were luxury passenger seats for Philip and me. Of course, we never actually became airborne, but the realistic manner in which he revved up with deep, guttural, spluttering sounds and his warning of 'Now then, we're off, hold tight!', made me think that, perhaps, we might. Only occasionally did I worry about whether the hay aeroplane would remain intact when we soared up into the bright blue sky, or whether bits would drop off all round us as we zoomed over our house with our bowler-hatted pilot, pipe in mouth, calling a cheery greeting to Hilda, his daughter, as she hung out the washing in the back garden below.

There was Force for tea on those Monday afternoons. It stood in the centre of the table, a big packet from the shop, with a picture of Sunny Jim ready to leap 'High O'er the Fence' on the outside of the cereal packet.

There was relative calm while Mother was living in her own house. When it was too nasty to go out for a walk she loved to sit us on the table with the gramophone, then wind it up and play dance tunes on it for us. Then both Grandma and Grandad Taylor became 'none too cracky' and, regretfully, we left our happy little home and took up residence in the small stone cottage down the yard where the old 'Jam Factory' stood. That belonged to the shop too. An electric bell was installed in our parents' bedroom, so that when John or Jane required attention in the dead of night Joe would hear the alarm bell, leap into his trousers and race across to the shop.

One Saturday morning after his first stroke, Grandad 'Shop', a keen football supporter, was in bed knocking at death's door according to Grandma, and the doctor had more or less pronounced him a goner. But old habits die hard. It was Saturday afternoon, and Town was playing at home. He'd never been late for kick-off for years. The match was far more of an incentive to get well than any medicine. The spirit beat the flesh, and out of bed he clambered, much to the consternation of everyone concerned. A quick shave with the pepper pot,

Grandad Taylor and Philip

mistakenly grabbed for his shaving stick – he shaved downstairs
in the kitchen, it being warmer – and off he shot through the
shop door and down the road to the match. Grandma was sure it
would kill him, but it didn't. It did him good. Philip and I were
certain that the pepper pot incident had been enacted solely for
our amusement. It was impossible that Grandad could ever die.
Be ill, maybe. But die, never. Who would see to the shop then?

CHAPTER NINE

A SALE IN THE KITCHEN

Like many a creaking gate, Grandad lived on some years after his first stroke. Around the end of January they always had a sale in the kitchen. A notice was pinned in the window reserved for drapery, and it activated slippered, shawled and pinafored village women into a state of excitement.

Grandma was one of the old school, and everything in her shop could be relied upon to be of the very best quality, with scrupulous fairness as to price. But there was no tick, and no diddling either. In the early thirties she still wore long black dresses reaching her ankles, and, except for evenings and Sundays, a black pinafore patterned with polka dots and edged with dark red binding. With her pale honest face devoid of make-up, and hair gripped into a bun at the nape of her neck, she seemed to epitomize straightforward, honest trading.

Few ventured to take a rise out of Grandma, except maybe old Lil Thorpe, who had known her since girlhood and still took a fiendish delight in poking fun at her. One Saturday evening before the sale began on Monday, Grandma had been busy putting everything ship shape in order to devote all her time to the shop. Lil, wearing the inevitable squashed brown felt hat, dingy, shapeless tweed suit, and scraggy fur slung round her neck, popped in for a few odds and ends. She gave a derogatory glance around.

'Ah see tha's weshed t'shop floor agin lass,' she sniffed. 'It wor only t'other day ah saw thi down on thi hands and knees afoor. Ah 'spect you'll have had yer dinner off it today then?'

Grandma Taylor (tallest, in fur) on an outing with Annie Brummit (also in fur), *c.* 1930

The accompanying smile was insincere. A leer not unlike a werewolf.

Grandma wasn't to be riled. She'd always been more than a match for Lil. 'Aye, mebbee we have – an' tasted a lot better than it would off some folks' tables too.'

Lil bristled visibly. 'An' yer'll have starched all yer stockings, and yer John's socks be now ah suppose?'

Grandma, much as she disliked some of her 'queer customers' as she termed them, always managed to control herself. She knew it wasn't good for the business to lose her temper.

Sometimes I was allowed to help prepare the sale. Grandad, businesslike in stiff starched white collar and winged bits under his chin, white apron and shiny-backed waistcoat, showed me how to make price tickets. Neat oblong cards had to be cut from large sheets of white cap paper, which was used for wrapping bread. The price must be pencilled on clearly. If stockings were marked at 1*s* 11½*d*, then a line would be struck through the ½*d* sign. But I had to make quite sure that it still showed beneath. That was the price of thick woollen or lisle stockings, black ones, grey ones – the drabbest of the lot I thought – and a muddy beige, all housed in shiny white cardboard boxes in 'The Fittings' in the back room. Grandma kept one box for her better-off customers, at the prohibitive price of 2*s* 11½*d*.

Customers were of a more practical bent in those days, probably because most wives stayed at home and relied on their husband's wages alone. They bought serviceable printed cotton and drill working aprons, and were delighted if they could save the odd copper or two. So they stocked up on warm fleecy liberty bodices for their children, sturdy woollen knee-length hose for the lads, and combs – short for combinations – for themselves. Men rarely came in for their own underwear if they had wives or mothers. And oh the embarrassment if Grandad happened to be behind the counter when drapery for female customers was required! After much hedging around and desultory small talk about the weather, the customer came to the point.

'Is . . . er . . . t'missus in, Mr Taylor?'

'Aye.'

'Could ah speak to her a minute – private like?'

She was ushered into the inner sanctum, the back kitchen, with the utmost courtesy and ceremony, the door held open while she entered, then closed deferentially when inside. Here she could browse among all the drapery kept in the huge drawers along the back wall. Grandad retreated into the shop, where, if no other customers awaited him, he busied himself weighing up a few pounds of flour or sugar – anything to rid his mind of the image of what was going on at the other side of the door. There have been occasions when he forgot and went into the back, and a shawl had to be hastily thrown over a partially clad figure.

Grandma displayed some of her drapery wares on the big scrubbed table which we ate off, and which displayed the family Bible and picture postcard album on Sundays. What wares there were! Voluminous flannelette nightgowns fashioned to keep out the fiercest winter wind (and Yorkshireman!); grey fleecy lined bloomers which fastened with a button at each knee and sported a broad band at the waist; heavy and hairy woollen vests with sleeves (one would need to be strong to support the weight to begin with); and pale pink corsets fastened with busks and girded with steel bones to keep the feminine Yorkshire form in trim. They were often as much as 6s 6d a pair. But women, I'm sure, could have withstood even the Crusades in those, and returned home without so much as a scratch.

Grandma and Grandad Taylor in the back
garden of Central Stores, *c.* 1930

There were also mobcaps to cover steel curling pins while
work was done, artificial silk blouses with tiny pearl buttons for
'best', essential but dull-looking dishcloths, and plain white tea
towels, perhaps with a red border round or the words 'Tea
Towel' printed diagonally across.

Selecting the right size of shirt for husbands and fathers was
not the hazardous hit-and-miss affair employed today. Grandma's
customers first measured their husbands' necks with a piece of
string, cut it to the correct size, then brought it along with them.

Sometimes, if the sale in the kitchen was going well, Grandma
felt inspired to put the big black kettle on the fire, slice a currant
teacake into 'soldiers', and spread it thickly with fresh butter.
With special, favourite customers, they would have a 'bit of a
tea-party' while deciding what to buy. Often on those late
January afternoons, with snow softly falling, and blue willow-
pattern teacups full of steaming tea, many a heart was gladdened.
They knew that if they'd bought a bargain from Grandma there
would be no question of finding a fault and having to take it
back. It'd be right.

CHAPTER TEN

THE YEAST MAN

I often heard my grandparents refer to some of the hawkers who used to call at the shop in their early years. Cockle Harry sold delicious kippers for 2*d* a pair; his wife was called Fish Jane. Then there was Tin-Armed Bill, who, they said, was a hermaphrodite, though how they knew I shall never know. He never bought any underwear from them. Perhaps it was his squeaky, womanish, high-pitched voice that led to conjectures. However, he managed quite well with the hook he had instead of a hand to carry the wicker baskets containing his wares. That would be around 1905 or 6. Another fellow went round the village calling 'Crumpets, muffins, pikelets', vying to be heard with a chap who sold clothes props, carrying a whole load over his shoulder. Then there was always the call 'Rags-a bones-a bottles today?' and the clatter of horses' hooves down the cobbled street.

The only hawker I remember, besides the pot man who clanked round on Monday afternoons, was the Yeast Man. He wasn't, I suppose, the kind one would describe as 'A Grand Chap'. Neither was he a bad chap. He was simply an unobtrusive thin little fellow who never claimed to be anything else. But to the shop, Alf was an institution. When Grandad was a young man, starting in business on his own, Alf was a young man too, and already hawking yeast to make a living.

When I was small, Tuesday was the Yeast Man's day. We had moved back to the shop by this time. Alf appeared as regularly as clockwork at about twelve o'clock and sat down on the springless black horsehair sofa in the back room without a word. There was always something strangely fascinating to me in Alf's faraway, watery-blue eyes.

'Will you have a cup of tea Alf?' Mother asked, hand ready on the large brown earthenware pot.

'Aye – ah don't mind.'

Question and answer never varied. Having thus cautiously assented to the invitation, Alf would sit motionless, balancing his white cup and saucer on bony, pointed, yeast-scented knees, in an oddly genteel manner.

Winter and summer alike, the Yeast Man came clad in his threadbare suit of greyish cloth, and flat, dun-grey cap, which he wore plumb on his head. Never did I hear him complain about the vagaries of the weather, or of anything else for that matter. His life, his clothes, his whole horizon, even the very air he breathed, was bound up with yeast.

Alf Dyson, the Yeast Man, who visited the shop on a Tuesday

One very bad winter, deliveries to the shop were badly delayed by a great snow. Grandad wondered anxiously whether there would be enough flour, sugar and so on in the big bins in the bakehouse to continue baking that week. He also wondered about the yeast. By that time most of the goods were bought from wholesalers and large firms, but Grandad refused to tell Alf that he needn't call anymore. Some of the old-timers had a bounden loyalty to those who were with them at their small beginnings. Besides, Tuesdays wouldn't be the same without that peculiar yeasty aroma which lingered in the back room hours after Alf had gone. Anyhow, on that particular Tuesday dinnertime we had reached the bread pudding stage, and there was still no sign either of a delivery van or of Alf.

'He'll nooan come this weather,' said Grandad. 'It isn't fit to turn a blessed dog out, let alone an old feller like Alf.'

Even the customers who popped in every half hour or so, regulars who lived nearby and made it a habit to forget something so they had an excuse for another natter, couldn't bring themselves to 'nip across to John's' on a day like that. Then the shop bell tinkled.

'I'll go,' offered Mother.

In a couple of seconds she was back, beaming all over her face. She was followed by a scarecrow-like figure in flat, ancient cap, threadbare suit, and torn, dripping old raincoat. It was Alf. His

John Taylor standing in the doorway of the shop. Alf Dyson is in the middle of the road, with a basket on his arm

only other concession to the bitter weather was an orange and brown striped muffler knotted round his scraggy throat.

'Ee lad, tha should ne'er a' turned out i' this lot,' reproved Grandad, but with a look of boundless admiration for his old friend.

Alf hung up the raincoat on the door knob, sat himself and his basket of yeast down on the couch, and wiped a droplet from his red, pinched nose.

'Ay, it's nooan sa bad if yer nobbut keeps gooing,' he replied, the pale blue eyes watering more than ever.

When it came to the test, a little insignificant chap like Alf could beat those enormous delivery vans!

'Will you have a cup of tea Alf?' fussed Mother, poking the fire into an even bigger blaze. I half expected fanfares to suddenly bugle out into a heartfelt rendering of 'See, the Conquering Hero Comes'. Alf thawed, verbally as well as physically.

'Aye, ah don't mind if ah do.'

Had I imagined it, or did the expressionless voice hold a shade more eagerness than usual? Anyway, in that terrible week in early February the bread for the villagers was baked as usual. Thanks to Alf, the little Yeast Man. It's heartening, when you come to think of it, what a lot of folk will go on doing the job, come fair weather or foul. Alf was one of them.

CHAPTER ELEVEN

SAT'DAY MORNING

At our village shop, Saturday morning was something special. To Grandad especially, it was a challenge to his capabilities as businessman and organizer of his customers' weekend bread supply – a challenge not undertaken lightly. Sadly, in his later years he always fell short of his ideal, of a Saturday morning running to plan and not ending in total confusion. Nevertheless, he woke to each new Saturday morning knowing it offered a fresh testing time. Prompt at 6 a.m. 'T'Owd Lad', as he had become known to one and all, even his elderly and most loyal customers, would rush across the linoleum-covered landing to Dad's bedroom, rapping urgently on the door.

'Joe, Joe! It's Sat'day morning lad,' was the never-changing bulletin, his voice a mixture of agitation, optimism and impatience. 'Nah then cum on lad, get up. There's all them there bread orders to see to tha knows.'

By that time, Dad was Grandad's right-hand man in the business, and we had moved in to live with them at the shop. On Saturdays the whole family rallied round, and even Mother forgot her dancing lessons and lent a hand.

This once-a-week all-out drive to get the customers' bread orders correct certainly motivated everyone to pull their weight. All donned spotless, starched white aprons and helped Grandad. But it didn't make one iota of difference. Somehow, between

The Co-op at Mirfield, near Huddersfield. The Co-operative Society was the main rival of the private grocer

them, they always ended up in a hopeless muddle. Either they were so many loaves and teacakes light or they had umpteen to spare at the end of the morning. Customers liked to get their bread in before dinnertime, to leave the afternoon free for other things. If the disaster was that enough bread hadn't been baked – or inadvertently sold to someone who hadn't ordered any – either Philip, my brother, or I were dispatched to neighbouring establishments to try and purchase extra of whatever was required. Never did we go to the Co-op. That would have been sacrilege. No private trader worth his salt would stoop to such practices.

Once the main customer's order had been collected and paid for everyone breathed a sigh of relief. Mrs Griffiths, the coalman's wife, ordered the same items week after week, year after year. Woe befall an assistant who questioned her right to the exact order. Even if there had been an earthquake she would still expect, and demand, half a dozen currant teacakes, two brown loaves, and one white.

If there wasn't spare bread anywhere else in the locality Dad had, on occasion, to 'fiddle' the orders, as he termed it. A brown

Joe – the right-hand man in the shop

loaf sneaked from the parson's order – he could be relied upon to understand and not make a fuss – or a white one 'nabbed' from somebody else's, and a couple of teacakes from old Fred's, who never remembered what he had ordered in any case. Sometimes it was realized, too late, that it was Mother who was the culprit, having put too much bread away in 'The Fittings' at the back for home use. Or that 'someone' (Grandad) had been using the wrong spectacles and read fifty for sixty the night before. Whoever the culprit, they couldn't escape the scathing adjectives that 'T'Owd Lad' could mete out when a Sat'day morning went wrong. A man of upright character, neither given to drinking, smoking nor swearing, and a superintendent at chapel, the miserable offenders would be either 'Blockhead', 'Toerag' or plain 'Fathead'.

Try as one may, something always seemed to go wrong on Saturday mornings. There was the traumatic moment when Grandad disappeared beneath the floorboards at the back of the counter. One minute he was there, wrapping bread, the next he'd gone – while attending to one of his most prized customers too. To add to the confusion, it was a Christmas Eve, and there were mince pie orders and Christmas cakes to attend to into the bargain. Would there now be a body lying in state in the front room over Christmas, Dad wildly imagined as he dashed, distraught, into the cellar. How was he to know that the floorboards were rickety and ready to give way? Mother, shaken, remarked to the dumbfounded customers as Dad disappeared as well, 'That's a bit of a beggar!' However, to everyone's utter amazement, the old man, none the worse for his sudden and undignified removal from the scene of action, was standing among the soap boxes and cardboard cartons in the cellar, scraping bits of plaster out of his ears. Only his forehead was wrinkled in anxiety.

'How's t'bread orders going Joe lad?' he queried.

When the final customer had gone, Dad always shoved any left-over bread into an old potato sack. It would always sell off cheap on Monday morning to Mr Truelove, who kept ferrets, hens and a donkey.

There were no such things as freezers then to keep bread in over the weekend. These days, in the streamlined efficiency of supermarkets, calculators and computers, everything is so orderly about Saturday morning shopping.

And yet, though brisk and efficient, be that as it may, the large firms will always have two endearing qualities missing: the personal touch, though it was often prone to human failing; and the humour that one could always be sure of finding in our little village shop. After all, the unpredictability of finding you've inadvertently been given Mrs So-and-so's large brown or Mr Thingumajig's currant sliced, beats all the dehumanized orderliness that we have to put up with today.

CHAPTER TWELVE

HYMNS AND BLACK JUICE

I wouldn't swap the chapel- and Sunday school-dominated Sundays of my childhood for the stuck-in-traffic jams ones many children take for granted today. Every Sunday morning during the thirties and early forties, spring, summer, autumn and winter alike, schoolfriends Betty and Leslie knocked at our back door to see if Philip and I were ready for Sunday school. Blue 'star' cards in hand we set off, happy as larks. Another star was stamped on our cards, adding up to a book prize for 'Regular and Punctual Attendance', a bit like motorists now get vouchers for glasses and soup bowls – an incentive to keep going.

It was enjoyable to sit in a semicircle, with the teacher reading stories of Jesus to us, proudly glancing occasionally at our best dresses of taffeta, crêpe de Chine, satin or checked gingham, clean white tennis socks and black patent shoes. There was also the feeling for the collection threepenny bit in our pockets, to make sure it was safe until the plate was passed round, and the hymn-singing, such as 'Jesus wants Me for a Sunbeam'. As we grew older there was sometimes the thrill of a love letter being handed to us behind the backs of other children from one of the boys. 'Will you go for a walk with me in the rec (recreation field) after? Love, Derek.' That type of thing; very secretive, very exciting.

The atmosphere of 'purity and being good above all else' must have ensured that nothing untoward went on in those walks in

Leslie and Betty Moorhouse, who used to
call at the shop and go to Sunday school
with Philip and Hazel

the rec, because even the most ardent lover never went further
than gently squeezing one's hand!

Then it was home for Sunday dinner, past open doorways, from
which came the steam and appetizing aromas from roast beef, cabbage
and Yorkshire puddings, wafting on the air. Philip and I changed into
second-best clothes to eat our dinner and read our comics.

Walter, the newspaperman, was usually propped up against the
living-kitchen wall adjoining our shop, having a refreshing drink
of Ben Shaw's lemonade or Tizer before continuing on his round.
His open sack, dumped on the pavement in front of the shop, and
guarded by Prince, our collie, who took it upon himself to do the
Sunday paper round with his pal Walter, was as safe as houses.

How enticing those papers looked – *The Empire News*, *Sunday
Pictorial*, *Sunday People*, coloured comics like *Rainbow* and *Tiger
Tim*, the pale blue *Funny Wonder*, and *Chips*, printed on paper
the colour of washed-out ladies' bloomers, *Laurel and Hardy*, and

the others shared our dinner table, propped up against glasses of pop. My idea of Heaven was to snatch *Tiger Tim* first, prostrate myself on the black horsehair sofa, and avidly turn the pages while dinner was served up.

Betty, Leslie, Philip and I usually walked the fields way home from afternoon Sunday school, leisurely picking bluebells in the neighbouring woods in summertime. We were always warned by mother to stick together, but though there were a few 'characters' in the village, none would have done us any harm. They too had been to chapel for the service which took place when Sunday school finished, and knew that God was watching over them, and that they'd better behave!

Hazel and her mother in 1937. Hazel's dress was made by the local dressmaker, Miss Atkinson

Sunday evenings meant chapel for Mother and Dad. The only deviation in our regular routine was being shared between our two sets of grandparents. One week we stayed with the shop ones, the next at Mother's parents. Grandma Taylor had strict rules. Every time the clock struck the hour Philip and I were invited to choose one liquorice torpedo from the small bag. The games of ludo and snakes and ladders continued until Mother and Dad returned from chapel.

We were always taken down to the other grandma's, to make sure we arrived safely. Grandad Haigh went to chapel too, but Grandma stayed at home, because of her bad legs and us.

Winter Sabbaths were best. We were ushered in at the door, past the dark overcoats in the tiny entrance, and the baleful stare of the stag's head which kept a sternly permanent watch over the hats and coats. Uncle Willie didn't care a hoot about the sanctity of that stag. When he visited he chucked his bowler hat and white muffler on to its antlers. I don't know how he dared.

The one large room was covered in plum-coloured coconut matting, and lit by a central gas mantle which plop-plopped uncertainly throughout the evening, shedding a dull yellow glow over the crimson plush tablecloth. Periodically, Grandma rose from her chair to pull one of the flimsy chains in an effort to heighten the barely adequate light. A dark oak sideboard, triple-mirrored, stood imposingly opposite the Yorkshire range. If Grandma, Philip and I stood together there looked to be quite a crowd reflected in the mirrors. A pair of bellows waited in a corner of the fireplace, ready to blow life into the fire again next morning. Even in summer, a fire was kept going all day to keep the oven hot. A pint pot, criss-crossed with tiny cracks of age, contained thick black Spanish juice, which Grandad Haigh swore by to keep his bowels moving. Nobody risked drinking much of that on dark, frosty nights, because it was dangerous down 'those awful steps' and across the back yard to the privy, according to Grandma. If there wasn't a moon, we might also get into the wrong one by mistake, if a neighbour had forgotten to lock it. Each privy owner had a long key, a bit like gaolers use, and finding the lock if it was pitch black and pouring with rain was a tedious job. Grandma's key was kept on a bit of string hung behind the back door. What a nuisance if one rushed out in a big hurry and forgot it. What temptation to sneak into an open door, even if it belonged to Mrs Kimberlain or another neighbour!

The three ladies who shared the yard vied with each other as to who kept their little outdoor retreats the cleanest. The 'thorough' clean was done on Friday mornings, with a generous swish of Jeyes' disinfectant to finish off with and new squares of newspaper hung on the privy nail to serve both as reading matter (with the door daringly left open an inch or two) and for toilet use.

Never a Sunday evening went by without Grandma's treasure chest unfolding its souvenirs of black-edged memorial cards and photographs of long-dead ancestors. Then the solemn sepia faces were re-interred in their coffin until next time as the clock ticked round to seven.

When it came to hymn-singing time, Grandma fancied herself as a conductor. A school ruler swished the air, nearly sending the gas mantle flying as she launched into 'Throw Out the Lifeline, Throw Out the Lifeline, Someone is Sinking Today-ay'. Her father had been a sea captain in Sunderland, and an ancestor had been an interpreter and sea captain too. In the French Court he met and fell in love with one Countess Le Normande. They married and came to live in Sunderland. We listened to that wonderful story every fortnight, proudly being informed that we had blue blood in our veins. One Sunday evening Philip produced a penknife and tried to find out!

Finally, there was cocoa and buttered oatmeal biscuits for supper. Around eight, our parents, looking holy and righteous till next morning, arrived, with Grandad still smoking his pipe.

'Did the parson preach a good sermon?'

'Aye, not bad,' replied Dad.

'Was it a good anthem?'

'Lovely,' replied Mother.

Then it was on with coats, caps, hats and scarves, kisses all round, and the walk back up to the shop, while the peace of another Sabbath evening softly enfolded us.

CHAPTER THIRTEEN

TRAVELLERS' TALES

On Monday mornings we were awakened by the thunderous bangings at the shop door of the flour men, accompanied by Prince's frenzied barking. It was one of Dad's failings that he never could get up when the alarm clock rang, so more often than not the first callers of the day were received by him in his sleeping shirt. No longer a slim youth, Joe rapidly acquired a 'corporation' and became a roly-poly bundle of fun and laughter, except on the occasions when Mother's flirtatious nature overstepped the mark. There was the time, for instance, when the new young parson had been invited to the shop for Sunday dinner and tea. During the afternoon Mother managed to be upstairs in the front room with him, ostensibly to hear him reading passages of the Bible to her while Dad washed up downstairs. But he crept upstairs on all fours, so Mother would not hear him, and flung the front room door open to find Mother and the dog-collared parson in a passionate embrace.

'If that's what you call religious instruction you can take it elsewhere!' he stormed, and the parson went downstairs far quicker than he had gone up.

However, like so many other similar incidents, it passed over, with Mother dismissing it as 'just a bit of fun'. And because Dad still preferred Mother and her bits of fun to anyone else, the union continued.

Dad thought it politic to deal with more than one flour firm, so patronized both Dyson's and Sugden's. One particular Monday it was Sugden's men who had Dad leaping out of bed to unbolt the shop door. One of the flour men, with thickly-floured white eyelashes, face, hands and eyebrows, scooped me up and playfully chucked me up toward the rolls of ham hanging from the ceiling. It was too much for Prince, who sprung to my defence and dug his teeth into the fleshiest part of the fellow's anatomy, which meant that the floury apparition was brought down to earth sooner than I was. His reaction was quite unexpected, and truly magnificent, after Dad managed to pull Prince away.

'He did quite right, he was only doing his job,' the flour man panted.

He soon recovered his composure after a cup of tea in the kitchen and a couple of digestive biscuits. As he drank, tiny beads of perspiration trickled down his forehead, making small pathways down the white flour. Then Mother divested him of his ripped dungarees and stitched them together with bright red cotton.

'There,' she announced, putting the last stitch in, 'not very professional, but you'll look bright and breezy in them now.'

She always chose red cotton from the drawer in the shop, no matter the colour of the garment to be mended. She couldn't resist bright colours.

Allinson's flour traveller kept more civilized hours. A Jew from Leeds, tubby, with twinkling brown eyes and a flamboyant disregard of his faith's food taboos, he endeared himself to us all from the start. Although obviously having plenty of money, plus a smart and sophisticated wife, he fitted in perfectly with the by now 'rough and ready' regime that reigned at the shop. He timed his visits for dinner, arriving in a comfortable car. First there was the tinkling of the shop door bell, then a cheery 'Stay where you are – it's only me'. Then Maurice, as he asked us to call him – he couldn't abide formalities – appeared in the kitchen doorway. An expansive, dimpling smile, balding head, beautifully cut suit over an expanding girth, and the inevitable cigarette drooping between nicotine-stained fingers. Whether Dad was present or not, he made a beeline for Mother, enveloping her in a great bear hug, while flicking his elegant cigarette case open for Dad to help himself.

'What's cooking SA? Be a darlin' and fry me a bit o' bacon and egg.'

An advert for Sugden's flour

Sometimes I came in from school while he was in the kitchen, nosing round Mother and the Belling electric cooker.

'What's SA mean?' I asked.

The only reply I received was 'Come on Hazel, give us a kiss. You'll learn some day!', accompanied by a huge wink in Mother's direction.

As I submitted to the wet kiss plonked on my lips I wondered if any of my friends would be having such an unusual aperitif before their dinner. Later, on our way back to school, Philip told me scathingly, 'SA stands for sex appeal, you ass.' I wasn't any wiser.

Mother's SA didn't have to rely on any artificial aids such as peroxide hair. Hers, naturally black, was washed with Amami for Brunettes and she had it marcel-waved. It contrasted vividly with the specially made military-style overalls she favoured during shop hours, wearing a different pair each day, with different coloured collar and cuffs. Her appeal, apart from her quite outstanding good looks, was her bubbling vivacity, sense of humour, and ever-ready willingness to provide refreshments for anyone, especially the travellers who visited the shop.

The Taylor family in the 1930s

Maurice's day was Wednesday, half-day closing. That gave him plenty of opportunity to chat over his bacon, eggs, tomato and HP sauce, and, if it was a pleasant afternoon, to take Mother and Dad for a 'run' over the moors in his car. This meant he could combine business with pleasure, as he called at outlying shops. Maurice enjoyed having someone to talk to between calls at isolated places.

We never had a car. There was never any time for Dad to learn to drive, so the most we ever achieved on wheels was the sack cart, a long, iron contraption on a couple of wheels, with rungs at intervals and long handles. It was used for delivering orders. We thought we were tycoons when we eventually acquired a bright blue kind of enclosed box on a couple of wheels, with a long handle to push it. Across one side, in gilt lettering, were the words 'J. Taylor, Grocer, Central Stores'.

Sometimes the Wednesday afternoon jaunts with 'Allinson's' went as far as Nont Sarahs, Halifax or the Wessenden Valley. One afternoon Dad was too involved with paperwork to accept

Maurice's offer of a run out. Mother wasn't. She changed into her black skirt, vivid red blazer with brass buttons down the front, and slunk into the house after the drive with a suspicious-looking swelling on her lower lip.

'Just a bit of a cold sore I'm getting,' was her excuse when it was mentioned. But the truth was that the flour traveller's ardour for his beloved SA had overstepped the normal limits of customer–traveller relationships as they halted for a while on the Yorkshire moors. He'd bitten her too hard.

Maurice admitted he had a 'right cushy' job. If the weather was bad, he remained in the comfort of his home and telephoned for his orders. One lovely hot Sunday afternoon Mother, Dad, Philip and I were invited to his home for tea. How astonished we were when his wife produced home-made ice cream to accompany the luscious strawberries. Hardly anyone in the thirties had a refrigerator. Stuff was kept cold in cellars. There wasn't a thing out of place in the beautifully appointed home, yet somehow or other we sensed an air of stifled boredom. This was confirmed when Maurice whispered as his wife went to the gleaming kitchen, 'It's not a patch on your bacon and eggs, SA.'

The Lyon's tea traveller was a wiry type, a bachelor who adored sport of all kinds, and frequently demonstrated a wrestling hold on Dad or Philip, much to their dismay. He drove up in a van which proclaimed on both sides what kind of animal he represented, then he sauntered into the kitchen, chain-smoking as most of the others did. His garb of office consisted of a pork pie-shaped trilby with a jaunty little red and green feather stuck in the hatband, a dark brown pin-striped suit, beige gabardine mac over one arm, and highly-polished brown shoes. Although he shouted 'Shop' when he entered, it still didn't stop him reaching the kitchen before anyone could attend to him. They all adored the easy-going camaraderie that existed back there, and the roars of laughter that seemed to punctuate conversations. Whatever we happened to be doing, he sprawled nonchalently on the old black horsehair couch and wisecracked his way through half an hour or so, pot of tea in hand, before reaching for his order book. I'll never forget the time he gave me a big annual for a Christmas present, and an equally big one for Philip.

Rarely did we have a dinnertime without a traveller of some description giving us the benefit of his experiences while refreshing himself with a pot of tea and a bit of cake. During the Spanish Civil War in 1937 'Lyons', as we called the tea traveller, became a sort of adoptive uncle to a couple of Spanish brothers, Roberto and Orellio. Philip was by then at the boys' college, and making excellent progress in Spanish language. He loved to swagger into the shop in his college uniform of black blazer with emblem on the top pocket, grey trousers and black cap with red stripes. There he would accost some humble customer with a quick-fire phrase or two in Spanish. The only reaction he ever had was open-mouthed astonishment and a, 'Nay lad, tha'd better speak i' plain Yorkshire if ah'm to understand thi.' Philip grinned broadly and replied 'Si, si, señorita,' or 'Si, si, señor.' They all thought he'd gone crackers.

Hazel with John Hall, the shop assistant, 1938

After witnessing one of those linguistic displays one Monday dinnertime, our Lyons traveller suggested that Philip may like to meet Roberto and Orellio and try out his skill on 'the real thing'. So it was arranged that Lyons and the Spanish boys should come to the shop for tea the following Sunday. I was greatly impressed by the physical attributes of the two young Spaniards, only having seen pallid English youths before. Beautifully smooth olive skins, flashing brown eyes and thick glossy hair. But oh, so shy.

We all waited impatiently for a brilliant conversation to develop over the boiled ham and piccalilli. Nothing happened. Lyons kept up a fluent monologue in impeccable Spanish, alternating with his usual broad Yorkshire witticisms. Philip uttered not a word, either in English or Spanish, so, tea over, the bagatelle board was brought out to make the language more universal.

There were, of course, some commercial travellers who were as dry as dust conversation-wise, and we never discovered anything about their personal lives. Some appeared week after week, without fail, for years, yet were so remote in personality – only really identifying with the product they were selling – that we could never allude to them by name. They were referred to as the Brasso Man, Tizer Chap or whatever.

Such a one was the bowler-hatted, starched white-collared, black-overcoated Parazone Man. His coat had a neat velvet collar, with never any dandruff on it – perhaps the Parazone dispensed with that. His throat had a dry cough, and he carried kid gloves and a briefcase. We always hoped his calls would be brief as well. He himself had no desire to fraternize longer than was necessary to take down his orders for the next delivery date.

'Have you owt fresh then, Mr er –?' Dad occasionally asked, as the bleating voice droned on.

'No, ah don't think ah have. Are you alright for Parazone this week Mr Taylor?'

Never Joe, as the matier ones called Dad. The Parazone Man's firm was old established and believed in deference to its esteemed customers. Mr Parazone looked out on the world of commerce from behind two worry lines which ran down his forehead, topped by his black bowler hat, and appeared bleary-eyed from his constant battle to clean up Yorkshire's homes with his firm's products.

'How about Silvo, Zebra Polish, Cherry Blossom, Stardrops? Fairy soap, donkey stones, Dolly Blue, Acdo, Rinso, Mansion Polish?'

The Parazone Man's recitation invariably ended with him raising his eyes hopefully from his order book and asking again, as though suddenly inspired, 'Parazone, Mr Taylor?'

Poor Mr Parazone must have felt awful sometimes, for when the shop bell tinkled and Mother or Dad rushed to the little window through which they could see who had entered, neither of them went. Each waited for the other to go and listen to the same old list. Dad had even been known to go to extremes, and to crawl beneath the big table out of sight in the kitchen until the Visitation had gone away. This would have been an unheard-of carry-on when Grandad and Grandma held the shop reins more tightly!

Cleansing agents for human Yorkshire interiors were bought from Henry Sykes, chemists: a bottle of Nurse Harvey's to bring up baby's wind, Fenning's Fever Cure – what bitterness stayed on the tongue after a dose of that – California Syrup of Figs to jolly along reluctant bowels, Beecham's powders or Pink Pills for Pale People. The gooey black, revolting syrup of figs was too handy for Mother. Even if one bottle was finished, there was no escape for Philip and me. There were rows and rows of it on the shop

Philip and Hazel on holiday in Scarborough, *c.* 1937

shelves. Every Friday after tea she poured a teaspoonful each for us. We hated it, and she had to sprint round the kitchen table holding it before her numerous times, spilling little black sticky drops on the way. Every week was exactly alike. The ritual never deviated. To shouts of 'Come here, you little Devil!', the three of us whirled round and round, beneath the table, into the shop, storming through customers without so much as an 'excuse me' to escape the spoonful of 'Black Hell'. Customers had many a laugh watching or listening to the performance. After we'd been caught and our noses held to prevent us from smelling, as well as tasting the stuff, we hurtled to the sweet counter with screwed up faces for something to take the taste away till the next Friday.

A favourite among the reps was Dimpling Duckworth, as he was known. He represented Hobson's, tobacconists. He seemed to be forever smiling. He had lovely laughing brown eyes, and dimples in his cheeks as big as quarries when he laughed, which he often did. Duckworth was always immaculately dressed in dark grey coat, pin-striped suit, white shirt, silk tie, homburg hat and gloves. He smelt delicious too. Mr Duckworth was on

Christian name terms with everybody, even many of our customers. The females went completely gaga if they came into the shop and he was there. Whoever was in his vicinity, be it slippered and curling-pinned housewives, workmen popping in for an ounce of twist, Mother or Dad, everybody was invited to have a cigarette. His elegant silver cigarette case flicked open and shut almost non-stop, and he did it with panache and style.

Mother never smoked at all until in her thirties, and the advent of the charismatic Dimpling Duckworth. Previously, she had considered women who smoked to be common. But one Christmas she succumbed to Duckworth's gift of Passing Clouds.

'Ooh, I can't resist the box!' she exclaimed. 'Will I look like a film star if I start smoking?' she asked, rolling her eyes provocatively.

'You look like a film star now darling,' was the reply.

One of the gift packets of Turkish cigarettes she received from him had the ends tinted in pretty pastel shades of pink, green and mauve.

'I'll match them to my garters,' she joked.

The traveller was then treated to a glimpse of satiny garters with a cluster of tiny pink rosebuds in the centre!

Another Christmas she was given Black and White Markovitch cigarettes, and kept the oval gold-coloured container for years. She kept some of her trinkets in it later on.

It made the younger housewives' day if they happened to pop into the shop when a young and dashing rep was there. They adored the unusual, courteous manner in which the gentlemen stood back to allow them to be attended to first, loved a joke with them, and, if they were lucky, and fancied, perhaps even a squeeze, kiss or free sample of some novelty or other. It may only have been a miniature bottle of scent or a few sweets, but they went off home as thrilled as if they'd been handed the crown jewels.

Bolder types made an excuse to burst into the shop again if hand-outs were in the offing.

'Our So-and-so's just called. D'you think you could spare another for her?'

They looked upon commercial travellers as all-year-round Father Christmasses, and if they were having a slack day at home, all the washing and baking being done, they sat on the upturned pop boxes and the bentwood chair kept in the shop for customers, and wasted half an hour gossiping and gazing with open-mouthed awe at the wares in the travellers' cases, listening to their tall stories, and promising faithfully to buy only their firms' products in future.

Central Stores took on something of the air of a 'palais de danse' at times. When the young women returned they'd have taken out their steel Dinkie hair curlers, fluffed their hair out, removed headscarves and pinafores, and dabbed a bit of cheap red Tattoo lipstick on. Sometimes there was an aura of Californian Poppy even, which wasn't discernable the first time they came in. (It was to be hoped their homecoming husbands imagined it was for their benefit!)

Regular orders were given for the working mens' cigarettes. Wild Woodbines in their pale green wrappings, Goldflake, Robin, Craven A, Players, and tins of twist. Thick Bulwark was a popular brand. Some bought it to chew on their way to work at the mill or ICI. Grandad Haigh used to stroll up to the shop to buy some on Monday afternoons. He let me roll it for him in the palm of my hand. It had a beguiling aroma. So had snuff.

Legally, children weren't allowed to serve in shops under the age of fourteen, but I could help to cut the coils of twist into half ounces. They reminded me of those eerie smoke snakes that ooze slowly out of a box on Bonfire Night.

On the sides of the house and shop were tin posters. For Colman's Mustard, The Bisto Twins, with noses cocked permanently in the air, Bovril, and Brooke Bond Tea.

Mother and Dad were so friendly with Dimpling Duckworth that one day they were invited to tea at his home. They spent the evening playing whist, smoking – of course – and drinking shorts. Mother enjoyed the unaccustomed sophistication up to a point, but she wasn't so hot at whist, didn't know how to inhale properly, and had to admit afterwards that she felt more at home with Tizer or dandelion and burdock than dry Martinis and suchlike. Dad enjoyed the change too, but he felt more natural with a pan full of mussels in front of him for tea, and the latest edition of *Magnet* to read and giggle over, propped up against the teapot.

That was his Monday treat, after Hopkinson's horse and cart had paraded down the road, pulling the cartload full of mugs, plates, earthenware bread crocks, basins with primrose-coloured insides, and chamber pots swinging from hooks. The Pot Man hawked mussels too. His bell clanged loudly and the vendor's voice boomed, 'Pots, pots!' Dad always gave old Ben, the carthorse, a carrot or two to help him on his way.

'I don't know how you can stomach those things,' Mother observed. She had begun to patronize a dancing school on Monday afternoons, Fox's of Trinity Street, for private dancing lessons in the tango, foxtrot and quickstep. As she was now sophisticated enough to smoke, she had decided to take up dancing to complete the daring new image. Her parting shot as she tucked the brown paper bag containing her silver dancing shoes under her arm was, 'Well, I'm off. Don't mussel yourself before I get back.'

He never did, and looked the picture of contentment in his clean white apron, dexterously picking the green bits out and whizzing them into the fire, while chuckling away at the latest exploits of Bunter, Bob Cherry, Harry Wharton and co, never even dreaming that his wife's future exploits would hold much more significance for him.

As it was, he trusted her implicitly, thinking that her little flirtations were, after all, only a bit of fun. He treated her more as an indulgent father would a child. If she was happy, then so was he.

The dancing school, where Hilda had private dancing lessons

CHAPTER FOURTEEN

SUNDAY SCHOOL SCHOLARS

Philip and I, like most of our friends, would no more think of missing Sunday school both morning and afternoon than we would have dreamt of playing truant from day school. Impetus to attend regularly was there in the shape of blue 'star' cards, which were stamped with a star each attendance. Book prizes were awarded for regular and punctual attendance, and we could get an additional prize if we also put in extra scripture lessons. I have one. On the frontispiece is the information, 'Deighton Methodist Sunday School. First Class. 77 marks. Presented to Hazel Taylor for Scripture Examination, March 1940.' I chose the book *Goodbye Mr Chips*. How I gloated over that first class bit!

Of course, I'd been going down the hill to Sunday school for years before I was old enough for the scripture examination. In retrospect, I suppose that Philip and I were good for sales at the shop. To be seen attending Sunday school regularly, and our parents chapel, gave an aura of respectability and fair dealing.

My first impressions of Sunday school were of miniature-sized chairs, in good solid wood, low hooks for coats and hats, bare wooden floors, and a huge painting of Jesus in the primary class, a little room off the main hall. Jesus's lean, sensitive hands were perpetually outstretched over a mixed group of small children, all dressed in their country's traditional robes, among them a very yellow Chinese child, a black boy, an Indian, and a fair-haired

English child. There were also a couple of woolly, stateless blonde lambs, looking up adoringly. In a big curved archway of script were the words 'Suffer the Little Children to Come Unto Me'. I used to look up at them, and wondered when I would be suffered, and if I'd have to go to Him on one of the trams that rattled us into town.

Near the picture was a roll of honour inscribed with the names of babies christened at Deighton. For Leslie Moorhouse, we children automatically substituted the name we knew him more intimately by – Titty Pa Pa. Why, no one knew. Philip was Taty-Pie, derived from the surname Taylor somehow or other. He hated it. Still, it was an improvement on Titty Pa Pa.

Little Betty, Titty's sister, hair cut in a neat fringe, with half an inch of regulation ear lobe showing beneath her woollen cap, knocked at the back door for us every Sunday morning at quarter to ten. Leslie, Titty Pa Pa, wore a short-trousered grey flannel suit with a clean white handkerchief prominent in the breast pocket, which was identical to Philip's. The boys' knitted knee-length socks sported yellow, red, blue or dark green stripes round the tops. School caps were perched on their heads, star cards held firmly in clenched fists, unless one or the other forgot theirs, and had to race back up the hill to fetch it. Sometimes Betty and Derek Walton called for us too. It was their dad, Albert, who rejoiced in his Sunday newspaper round.

Albert's get-up was the same, winter and summer alike. Shabby torn raincoat, flat check cap, shiny black suit complete with well-worn, shiny waistcoat, and his father's gold watch chain looped across the front. He propped up the kitchen wall about 11 a.m. each Sunday, to swap jokes and quaff a glass or two of lemonade, Tizer or dandelion and burdock. Then it was 'So long Joe lad', 'So long Hilda lass'. And 'So long lad,' from Dad till the next Sunday.

'Can we come in and have a read of *Tiger Tim*?' sometimes asked Leslie and Betty.

Tiger Tim's was 'bright and beautiful', and we all wanted it first.

'I bags *Tiger Tim*!' we all four tried to shout out first.

Mother supplied free glasses of pop to accompany the reading. We always had a quart bottle of pop on the table to accompany

Sunday dinner. It was easier than putting on the kettle to make tea or coffee. Then, when that was finished, it was the easiest thing in the world to nip into the darkened shop – because the blinds were down for Sunday – and bring out another. Mother thought they were all free. So did we I suppose, because no money ever changed hands when we wanted some.

The ordinary newspapers interested me for one thing only. Were there any Shirley Temple pictures in them? If so, it was out with the scissors and cutting the picture out to flour-and-water paste it into my scrapbook before Dad or Mother had a chance to see what was on the other side.

At about 3.15 p.m., when afternoon Sunday school was over, Betty, Titty Pa Pa, Philip and I walked home the long way round if it was fine. There was a huge swamp in the middle of the field at the back of our shop and we used to risk our Sunday shoes by going as near the water and mud as we dare, to poke the frogs and tadpoles in springtime, and to watch them jump. I wasn't too keen on baiting tadpoles and frogs, or in being in their vicinity.

Miss Chinn, an appropriate name, as her chin was the most prominent thing about her, never missed a chapel service for years, morning or evening, besides always being there to teach the Sunday school scholars. They said that she did have a young man in the First World War, but he had been killed and religion had filled her life ever since. I couldn't help thinking I'd rather have had the young man. Most of us were apprehensive about moving up into her class. A weekday teacher also, she had the knack of being able to promote immediate discipline by a mere withering glance. Her dreadful hats also helped, the angle of each one seeming to scream 'Don't do that!' or 'Don't you dare!' To be near those creations was to be cowed.

In chapel Miss Chinn always sat in the front row of the choir stalls on the contralto side. Older children were expected to go across the road after Sunday school to morning service in chapel, and any giggling, nudging, whispering, or sucking of chapel spice (mint imperials) was immediately and effectively silenced by a non-vocal rebuke from Miss Chinn. First of all the eyes 'held' the culprit, then the chin swayed slightly from side to side.

Then the forefinger of the right hand appeared out of a clenched fist. No more was required.

Her second in command, Miss Amy Pearson, sat next to her for donkey's years. They obviously did not go along with the idea that a change is as good as a rest. They never went away on holiday and I honestly believe they would have died sooner than miss Sunday school and chapel.

There were some at Sunday school who made it a pleasure to attend though. How I loved being in the Sunday school concerts when John Edward Varley coached the children. John Edward, as he was affectionately known, was ever gentle, ever smiling, with his eyes, as well as his mouth. And that seemed to make all the difference. He was a perfect Grandad to us all.

One Easter I was chosen to be dressed as a fluffy yellow chicken, and I'd to burst out of a life-like eggshell on the Sunday school stage. I was thrilled when someone sent a bouquet of spring flowers on to the stage at the end of the show. John Edward advanced towards me with the bouquet.

'For the chicken,' he announced proudly.

Another time, when about three years old, I had a solo to sing. My stage companion was my own little wooden horse on red wheels. The song went something like this:

Come along my gee-gee, now come along with me,
And we will go together, to the greenwood tree.
Where the birds are singing, warbling all the day,
There I'll decorate you, for the first of May.
Come along my gee-gee, let us go and play.

Halfway through the song, and my perambulations round the stage, disaster struck. I stopped in my tracks, lifted up the rear end of the horse, scanned the audience for dear John Edward, and then called out loudly, 'The veel's tum off!' I could not pronounce either my Ws or Cs, or Rs for that matter. That unscripted bit of entertainment brought the house down. The whole show came to a halt as John Edward rustled up hammer and nails from God knows where, leapt on to the stage, and did a repair job there and then. My performance then continued.

Deighton Sunday School Queen, 1933. Winifred Holmes is attended by Hazel (far right), Jean Poppleton (seated next to Hazel), Mary Pool (standing on the left) and Molly Dyson (far left)

Other highlights of Sunday school were the choosing of the Sunday school Queen and her attendants. How I longed to be Queen, and wear either the crimson velvet cloak or the royal blue one! Once I did attain the status of attendant, but I never managed to wear one of those glorious plush cloaks.

My white dress was made by the village dressmaker. It was the first time I'd worn a long dress and I felt very distinguished, but not when bits kept flaking off my white shoes and leaving a trail wherever I walked. I could have killed Mother for not making sure they were alright before I set off for my big occasion, and failed to keep up the sweet smile I'd been told to wear. Indeed, I felt on the point of exploding with wrath each time another bit fell off.

During the Second World War even Sunday school teachers became more sophisticated. Mrs Watson taught the older boys during that time. We all thought her elegance personified after the matter-of-factness and no make-up of her predecessors. She was a sort of combination of Marlene Dietrich and Mrs Simpson, the Duke of Windsor's wife, with Marlene predominating.

On Sundays Mrs Watson wore a smart black costume, a huge fluffy black fur slung nonchalently over one slim shoulder, with black court shoes and sheer nylons, which enhanced her shapely legs. A perky black hat with veiling and big black velvet dots almost obliterated her right eye, but the left eye twinkled enough to make up for the temporary absence of the other. Mrs Watson's high, Russian-type cheekbones were accentuated with powder rouge of a hectic pink shade, while her eyebrows were plucked into lines of perpetual surprise.

She was really surprised one Sunday afternoon when the boys in her class, who nearly all had a crush on her, yanked the form from beneath her as she was about to sit upon it with her legs elegantly crossed. Clouds of dust puffed up from the wooden floorboards and settled on to Mrs Watson's narrow black posterior. But she staggered to her feet,

Hazel in her Whit Sunday attendant's dress and flaky white shoes

taking care not to snag her nylons, grinned that wide, scarlet-lipped smile, and continued with her lesson. No wonder the boys all loved her!

CHAPTER FIFTEEN

T'CHAPEL ANNIVERSARY

Right up to the Second World War, we Yorkshire folk looked forward to 't'chapel anniversary' with as much enthusiasm as people now have for a holiday abroad. It was a highlight of the year. One would have to be damned near dying to miss it. Indeed, I used to think that some of the worshippers, in their new flower-decked hats, looked as though they were.

The anniversary always took place on the last Sunday in June. When Grandad was alive he wore a tall silk black hat, striped trousers, and black morning coat for the big event, plus a sober 'it's t'chapel anniversary' look in his pale blue eyes.

What a sense of security and continuity there was in life, before people started to drift away from villages! Aunt Annie remembered attending the same chapel anniversary when she was a little girl.

'It wasn't all the finery of the new clothes, or the hymns that absorbed my attention,' she used to say, 'but old Mr Collie's gold albert with the fancy drop. He sat in our pew, and I wanted to play with his albert during the service, but someone always smacked my hand if I tried to get near it.'

In Annie's childhood anniversaries Doris and Fanny were Sunday school teachers, and they couldn't afford a new costume every year, not even for the anniversary, for there were all manner of eventualities to put by for in those early years. However, they usually managed to buy or make a new blouse each, and perhaps stitch a length of bright new braid round the hems of their ankle-length skirts. Mr Bill Berry was one of the staunch chapel superintendents. Another regular at the anniversary was old Mr Dyson, the greengrocer, who had a Rip Van Winkle beard stretching to his thighs. It must have been very cosy on winter nights in bed, before the advent of electric blankets and sheepskin underblankets. The flamboyance was in the length, not the shade. That was pepper and salt, like his anniversary suit. Mr Dyson had a son named Jabez, and Annie used to wonder if he was the origin of the exclamation 'By Jabers'.

The first time I took part in the Children's Morning Anniversary Demonstration I was five years old. How important I felt to actually be sitting in the choir stalls, where the omnipotent Miss Chinn and all the other choir members usually sat. Every summer Sunday until that one in June had been taken up at Sunday school with practising hymns for the all-important anniversary. 'Summer Suns are Glowing, Over Land and Sea' was a hardy perennial. In my ignorance I fully imagined that half a dozen or so foreign red balls of fire were bobbing about over different parts of the world, while our personal English sun dazzled our eyes through the coloured leaded lights, causing tiny clusters of dust to dance around our hymn sheets.

The Children's Service was the most popular of the day. I loved to sing 'There's a Friend for Little Children, Above the Bright Blue Sky'. We were young enough to have no fears about meeting him too soon. However, a tiny thrill of apprehension ran through me as we sang 'Jesus Wants me for a Sunbeam, To Shine for Him each Day'. How demanding Jesus was. I really thought that one day I should be transformed into one, while varied interpretations were put upon the hymn 'O Give Me Samuel's Ear' by the boys.

I was captivated by the sheer poetry of those old hymns.

> By cool Siloam's shady rill
> The lily must decay
> The rose that blooms beneath the hill
> Must shortly fade away.

Perhaps I'm possessed of a natural morbidity, but I adored such passages as:

> And soon, too soon, the wintry hour
> Of man's maturer age
> Will shake the soul with sorrow's power
> And stormy passion's rage.

One supposes that the popularity of the children's service was the unpredictability of it, the inescapable surety that one or other of the scholars would be bound to forget a verse if singing a solo, or come to a faltering, tearful stop in the middle of 'Gentle Jesus, Meek and Mild, Listen to a Little Child'. At such moments, all the world seemed to wait poised, holding its breath, when there was nothing else forthcoming to listen to. Of course, no one showed appreciation by clapping on Sundays. Yet there was an almost audible sigh of appreciation from the congregation when a child earned the softly murmured words from a teacher, 'Well done!'

There were straw bonnets, Panamas, ribbons galore, tiny artificial flowers adorning brims of hats and hatbands, frills, puff sleeves, cape sleeves, smocking on dresses, new white tennis socks and black patent shoes fastened with buttons – and the smell of newness everywhere. The smell of carnation buttonholes on small boys' flannel suits, fresh fern, dabs of Ashes of Roses scent behind the older girls' ears, or a dash of eau de Cologne or lavender water. The crackle of a taffeta dress, the tears of a child in pink crêpe de Chine which shrunk in a sudden downpour on the way home, boys with slicked-back hair, glossy from their dad's Brylcreem, crisp white shirts and striped ties, unaccustomed shiny faces and knees, and cleaned-out ears.

Inside the chapel everybody showed off their new clothes. Goodness knows how we managed to keep our outfits secret for weeks on end, but it was a constant source of speculation beforehand.

My new clothes came from one of the wholesale drapers that Dad patronized. I loved going for them with Mother on a Wednesday half-day closing. Big white cardboard boxes full of dresses, underslips, and knickers to match. For schoolwear

Hazel, aged ten, wearing her new pink
taffeta dress and matching bow for
Whitsuntide

mother ordered three or four print dresses at a time, usually with
the demure Peter Pan collar and cuffs so popular in the thirties.
But for special occasions, gleaming satin was greatly coveted. I
remember the sheer Heaven of having a shell pink satin dress
when I was five, bought for the Sunday school anniversary in
which I had a solo to sing. It had five deep frills in lieu of a skirt,
and I made myself dizzy twirling round and round, watching the
frills fly out like a ballerina's dress. My pride knew no bounds
when I was seated right in the centre of the front row choir
stalls, where everybody could see me.

Evensong, and the afternoon service after that, tended to be a
bit dreary, with the sun slowly sinking in the West, and
everybody worn out with all the toing and froing to chapel three
times that day. There was also the rigmarole of changing out of
our new clothes into our second-best before our meals, then
back into the anniversary finery once more.

Occasionally, however, there came a moment of sheer delight. Such as the hushed, ethereal moment when young aspiring soprano Mary Barker, an inappropriate name if ever there was one, sang 'I wandered alone in a Strange Land'. There wasn't a single bored sniff or cough to disturb the utter beauty and sincerity of the performance. A similar moment of ecstasy was the playing on the organ of 'Solemn Melody'.

Yet even in such moments, stray thoughts of the anniversary tea waiting up at the shop kept interrupting the flow of the music. There would be gooseberry pie, and a 'cow' pie, the old Yorkshire name for a big baked custard, as yellow as a buttercup and freckled with nutmeg. There'd also be Aunt Emily and Uncle William to help us eat it all up. They were both slow walkers, and I did wish they weren't, so that we could begin the anniversary feast quicker. I wondered how it would be if stout ropes were tied round them, and they could somehow be hoisted up the big hill back home. But no, they were forever 'out of puff', and we had to be polite and walk with our guests.

The flowers were a great feature of Anniversary Sunday. In our back garden behind the shop, the bright red tulips once stood along the trim lawn like guardsmen waiting to greet Aunt Emily and Uncle William. In Grandad's day there wasn't a weed or dandelion in sight. In Mother's day there wasn't a tulip in sight!

Any of the congregation who happened to be 'taken short' during a sermon had to creep out on tiptoe to the back privy, which was located among the tombstones. Avid readers were a long time in returning, such was the lurid temptation of *The Empire News* or *Sunday Pictorial*, or whatever else dangled from a rusty nail on the cobwebby, whitewashed wall. If the door was left slightly open to allow a shaft of light to penetrate the hallowed spot, one could hardly blame interlopers who also needed to 'spend a penny' for barging in. Frequently, worshippers in best bibs and tuckers would be strolling up the chapel walk when a piercing 'Oi – hold on – hold yer hosses missus!' would be emitted from the privy at the top end of the graveyard, and the unwelcome intruder would come reeling out.

Anniversary Sunday was a big day for some of the corpses too. Flowers were brought sanctimoniously to their graves, perhaps

A chapel choir outing. Hazel and Philip are standing in the front row, Hilda and Joe are to the right

the only adornment they'd had since the Christmas wreaths. I could never understand why people whispered as they weaved their way in and out of the graves, searching for their own dead. I should have thought that a bit of noise would be welcome after the long silence of the week. Some people became quite agitated, pulling aside the overgrown grass to find the right grave on which to place the jam jar filled with fresh flowers from their gardens.

'Have you seen our Flo?' or 'Yer haven't come across Charlie have yer?' they queried, just as though the dead relations were deliberately hiding from them.

At fourteen all my interest became centred on an aesthetic-looking male who had left the village, but who had returned – as so many did – to celebrate the chapel anniversary. He'd be quite old then, about twenty-nine, and acted as a steward to take the collection. I first saw him in morning service, and dreamed of him all through the Yorkshire pudding and roast beef at home till it was time to rush back for the afternoon service, hoping beyond hope that he would be there again. Suddenly, I was hopelessly smitten for the very first time.

My heart seemed to bump even louder than the chapel organ as the long, lean fingers came nearer and nearer with the wooden collection box. Would they actually touch mine? Alas, rotten Jimmy Chapman snatched the box and pushed a button in before I'd the chance to linger with the handsome steward, who never so much as glanced at me. Or if he did, I missed it. All that dream-like day every hymn of praise was sung in worship of him. God didn't come into it at all.

Now, like many other village chapels, the one I attended is left derelict and abandoned. The handsome steward is dead. 'Cow' pies have been usurped by such delicacies as shop-bought cheesecake or 'instant bakes'. No more do aunts and uncles and other relations set aside the last Sunday in June for the chapel anniversary. To those who never experienced such an event, it can't seem much of a loss. But to those of us who knew them in their heyday, the loss is immeasurable. They were special days in the calendar, when we learnt to count our blessings, and name them, one by one.

Another occasion in the chapel calendar was the Whit Monday Walk. Some of the youngsters thought it marvellous – all that marching, shouting, and showing off round the village streets – but it was an event that warranted no eager anticipation from me.

Forty odd years ago I used even to pray that it would rain 'cats and dogs' so that 'they' would call it off. But 'they' were a hardy lot, and the sun, in the days of my youth, always seemed to blaze down on the Whit Monday marchers.

Grandad was an enthusiastic 'Chapeller', and I suspect that he had something to do with The Walk. He was so insistent that I join in.

How I hated it! The buns were invariably supplied by Grandad from our shop, which added to the boredom of the affair. There were plain Queen cakes in neat bun papers, done up with white icing and quarter of a cherry on top, or white icing tops sprinked none too liberally with coconut. (Grandma, to give herself a treat, used to slice the icing top off her bun, and lay it at the side of her plate as a titbit for when the plain bit was eaten.)

Whit Monday after Whit Monday buns of that type appeared on the long, scrubbed Sunday school tables, and just as regularly the Sunday school superintendent, and attendant cronies, appeared to do justice to them.

To return to The Walk. Everybody had to assemble outside the Sunday school promptly at 1.30. Our female teachers wore stout walking shoes, no-nonsense beige straw hats, and prim, twinkly expressions. The butcher, coalman, postman and milkman were almost unrecognizable, having exchanged everyday apparel for the splendid navy and scarlet uniform of the local brass band.

Should I feign illness before Whit Monday, perhaps a sniffle or a sneeze, I was dosed nightly with Fenning's Fever Cure and Grandad remarked that 'Tha mun be fit for t'walk o' Monday!'

Once or twice Mother made feeble attempts to provide me with fancy dress in which to compete for one of the prizes. One humiliating Whit Monday I emerged into public view as a fairy, wearing a pair of limp wings created from huge sheets of white 'cap' paper, in which used to be wrapped the customers' bread. A baking tin served for my crown; it sparkled with pieces of silver paper tucked round. They dropped off one by one, as the march progressed.

A big, hastily scrawled cardboard placard (torn from a margarine box) announced to the world in general that I was a fairy. 'We'll wave as you pass. We'll be listening for t' band,' Grandma smiled, as I set off dismally for the school.

I wished that customers – droves and droves of them – would converge at the shop at the exact moment the procession was passing. The premises were open for the duration of the procession in order that thirsts could be quenched with bottles of Tizer, lemonade, or dandelion and burdock.

How I loathed being stared at, and having to grin inanely all along the route, or be told that I was a 'sulk-pot'. But there it is. Some people are 'naturals' for processions. Some just aren't.

Down at the school, Big Girls and teachers busied themselves in forming children into lines. They then placed themselves at strategic intervals on the outsides. With a terrific clash, the band struck up and my feet shuffled unwillingly into the varying tempos.

Frequent halts were made at important places along the route, our shop being one of them. How my heart would thump as we thundered ponderously down the hill, nearer and nearer to The Great Stare.

The shop doorway was always jammed with people calling out to individuals in the moving mass, with weary marchers who had run into the dark interior of the shop for a 'sup' from the glasses already filled with pop for quick consumption.

Grandma set out stools and shop chairs – those bentwood ones, with holes punched in the seat – outside the shop. It was a bit like a garden party, without the flowers and the top hats. Grandma and Grandad wore freshly starched white aprons down to their ankles for the occasion.

Dorothy Carter, who won a 5s prize in the Whitsuntide fancy dress competition, c. 1937

Dad, grinning from ear to ear beneath his inevitable bowler hat, bawled indistinguishable remarks, while Mother made ducks' eyes at the bandsmen.

Many were the pointing fingers and craning necks, while desperately I attempted to slink by unnoticed, with knees bent to bring me lower than the Golliwog who marched in front of me. Or I would try to get by, shrinking behind a Red Indian's feathers. I felt so silly marching all that way for a cup of weak sugary tea, a couple of fish paste sandwiches, and a bun from our shop.

During the pause outside our shop the band thundered through a couple of rousing hymns. It was maybe 'Onward Christian Soldiers', followed by the one that goes 'Hark! hark! hark! while Infant Voices Sing'.

I could not help feeling more like a dutiful rat following the Pied Piper than a devout Christian child as the throng continued its noisy way to the Sunday school for tea. Here all and sundry were greeted with exclamations of admiration from the refreshment ladies; they were local women who attended the Bright Hour every Tuesday afternoon. Without exception they kept their hats firmly on their heads throughout the proceedings. Indeed, one hardly ever did see a Bright Hour lady without her hat.

After tea, it was off to the field for races for those whose feet could stand up to it after the afternoon's march. There was all the tenseness of the fancy dress judging, more communal

Philip and Hazel enjoying the sun in the 1930s

singing, a prayer and then, about nine – as the sun dipped below the horizon – the last stragglers drifted home.

Scholars had been treated to drinks of free lemonade and another bun each. Another Whit Walk had passed into memory. I would not be on view, publicly, until Whit Monday afternoon next year – and wasn't I glad!

CHAPTER SIXTEEN

OUR MAID ALICE

When the local elderly women who had helped out at our village shop since the year dot gradually seized up with rheumatics, my parents began to think about the advantages of having a live-in maid. Local newspapers had whole columns of 'domestics' advertised. There were agencies all over, especially in Barnsley and Doncaster, so one Wednesday afternoon, half-day closing, Mother and Dad decided to have a bus ride to Barnsley, more as a jaunt out than anything. While there they called in at an agency dealing with 'domestics', usually girls who had left school at fourteen. They were introduced to a girl named Alice, who they thought would fit in well. They came home full of excitement, with plans to convert the attic into a bedroom for our very first maid.

Frank, Dad's boyhood chum, was brought in to catch as many mice as possible from up there before Alice's arrival, and to bung up all suspicious-looking holes. One of our charwomen scrubbed the linoleum with Stardrops and strong disinfectant. An ancient dressing table with tip-over mirror was polished and the drawers lined with pretty flowered shelf paper. Brass handles were shined with Brasso, and a huge jug, white with big pink cabbage roses painted on it, was cleaned out and stood in a matching porcelain basin.

'This bit of curtain will do as a wardrobe,' said Mother. 'Alice will be able to hang her clothes behind it.'

The chintzy material hung from a brass pole across the far corner of the attic. The big double bed had rusty springs but the old flock mattress was hung out to air, and flannelette sheets hauled up the wooden stairs to cover it. An old satin eiderdown was the finishing touch. However, the *pièce de résistance* of the

Frank Walker, Hazel's dad's childhood pal,
who worked at John Lee Walker's and was
adept at betting on the horses

newly-created bedroom was a huge chamber pot, brought out of
retirement from our grandparents' days.

'I'll let Alice have my torch too,' Mother decided. 'Attics can
be a bit frightening, especially when you're still only fourteen.'

The torch was placed on the dark oak bedside pedestal, then I
was asked to bring up a few back copies of *Home Chat* and
Picturegoer, plus some comics of mine.

'Alice might sleep better if she has something to read first,'
reasoned Mother, jumping sky high at an ominous scratching
noise coming from behind the skirting board.

Despite all the preparations, we felt slightly mean that anyone
should have to sleep up there in the attic while we slept in
proper bedrooms. So Mother let the new maid have the luxury
of a colourful pegged rug from her bedroom, placed at the side
of Alice's bed.

It sometimes sounded as though a whole battalion of mice was
scratching and squeaking along the floorboards up in the attic

when we lay in bed. Nevertheless, Mother hoped that regular squirts of Izal would do the trick, along with daily visits to the attic by a couple of our numerous cats. But which, I thought, would be worse? Only noises, or visible corpses under the bed, especially if Alice was using the . . . . Oh, it didn't bear even thinking about!

'Young Alice will be so thrilled to have a room to call her own that she won't worry about a few mice,' said Dad. 'Why, at home she probably sleeps half a dozen to a bed, with all her brothers and sisters.'

True, I suppose. Heaven to one person is Hell to another, depending on your circumstances.

There was one great advantage of the attic. In summertime one could open the skylight in the roof, stand on a chair and see for miles across the fields and woods. Sometimes one could even see the tiny white-clad figures of the nurses over at the TB hospital, darting about between the beds, which were placed outside in good weather.

'It's to be hoped the germs stay there and don't come sneaking over our garden fence,' worried Mother.

How different it was in the 1930s for a young girl 'going into service'. Then, she was a 'domestic' or 'maid'. Nowadays she is a glamorous-sounding au pair. But 'Our Alice' would be really impressed when we showed her that skylight in her very own room. Leaving home to work a few miles away in another town was as adventurous then as working in another country is today.

At last the day dawned when mother and I went into town to meet our new maid. Alice and her pale, weary-looking mother were coming by bus from Barnsley. My first impression of Alice was of a thin, scraggy-looking girl with straight mousy-coloured hair (how appropriate). A curvy hairgrip drew the hair to one side in a quiff. Our maid-to-be hadn't a semblance of make-up, and looked pale as an uncooked loaf of bread. Her thin lips looked bloodless, her sharply pointed nose unfashionably hooked. Alice's hands were red and chapped, already coarsened by too much housework. She wore a crumpled navy serge skirt and white blouse, and carried a shabby attaché case. Her mother dithered forward to shake hands, drawing her eldest daughter with her.

'Now then Alice, here's your new mistress, Mrs Taylor. Be a good lass and do as you're told.'

Tears were perilously close. The woman sniffed into a hankie.

'I'm expecting again yer see Mrs Taylor. Ah wouldn't have sent our Alice away from home so young, but we need the extra, and it will be one less mouth to feed.'

Mother flashed her warm smile and put a comforting arm round the woman's shoulders.

'She'll be right as ninepence with me, now don't you worry. Let's all go and have a cup of tea and some hot muffins before you go back.'

Alice's face lit up with relief. She liked her new mistress on sight. Besides, at a grocer's shop there would be plenty to eat!

'I'll come home on my half day off mum. Give my love to the children.'

Alice waved happily until the bus drew away, as I held her hand and told her all about Whiskers and Clover, and the rest of the cats.

When we were back home, Philip, my brother, welcomed her by saying he'd teach her to play ping pong and she'd be able to listen to *Fu Man Chu* with us on the wireless on Monday evenings.

'Won't we have some fun?' giggled our new maid.

After that, Mother felt a bit inhibited about bringing up the little matter of her duties.

'Perhaps you'll be able to do a bit of washing-up as well, Alice,' she suggested. 'And clean the fireplace out in a morning.'

There could hardly be any nine to five hours with living in.

'Put it this way,' Dad helped out. 'If there's something to do you'll help, and if not, then you're free to take the dog for a walk, go to the pictures, or whatever you fancy.'

Alice soon acquired a nickname. John, the shop assistant, and Dad – and any other male – loved to tease the new girl, creeping up behind her if she was standing at the sink peeling potatoes, or pegging out clothes in the garden. But our new maid had been warned about men. And how she screamed, half with delight, half with fear, when tickled beneath her armpits. Her response was a shrill 'You Do!', and none of her assailants knew whether that was an invitation or a threat. So she became not Alice, but

'You Do'. Alice had a limited vocabulary, and soon these two words punctuated every other sentence, even to anticipating a bit of horseplay before it had even been thought of. But it was much more exciting than being at home in Barnsley, looking after her younger brothers and sisters. Sometimes Dad gave her a playful squeeze, calling her 'Old Tin Ribs'. Then her thin, black-stockinged legs skipped adroitly out of his reach. 'You Do!' she squealed, enjoying it all enormously, and holding a bread plate in front of her like armour plating. Oh, what hysterics there were when a particularly handsome commercial traveller sauntered into the back kitchen and patted Alice playfully on the behind. Grabbing Mother, or whoever was nearest, she swung round and round holding her apron, shrieking at the bewildered rep, 'You Do! You Do!'

On the evenings when Mother and Dad went with the free pass to the theatre (given for showing the week's programme in a prominent position on the shop counter) what fun we had with Alice, especially if a few of Philip's pals came in to play. After supper Alice usually went to her attic bedroom to put her steel Dinkie curling pins in. That was the cue for us to creep quietly after her as she climbed the twisting wooden steps. Leslie stayed in the attic while we switched off the light, before yelling, 'Alice, there's a ghost.'

Those were the dark wintry evenings when Alice's yells of 'You Do!' really were a cry from the heart – and from under the bed. Poor Alice was fighting for dear life among the blanket fluff that she'd forgotten to dust out. Leslie held her under the bed, telling her to pretend he was Clark Gable, while spindly legs flailed the air.

'I've only been teaching her a bit of judo, so she can look after herself,' he explained, as our hot and flushed-looking maid emerged.

'Me dad'll kill me if I get into trouble,' Alice declared as she dusted herself down.

Alice became an avid reader of cheap love story paperbacks, and the attic light stayed on late into the night. She wore an uncomfortable amount of ironmongery in her hair, all held together beneath a pale blue or pink hairnet. Despite the curlers,

The only picture of Alice, the maid, standing to the left of the lightbulb. Also in the picture, taken at Christmas 1937, are Hilda with Hazel on her knee, Winnie Halstead holding her son, Brian, Marion Haigh (seated) and Kenneth Halstead

wisps of straight hair usually stuck out beneath her beret, while the rest was as frizzy as could be.

After disturbing Alice and Leslie beneath the attic bed one night, Mother thought it high time young Alice was taught the facts of life.

'Has your mother told you anything,' she asked, 'about how you get babies and things?'

Alice's eyes were as wide as soup plates.

'No. Well, I know that you haven't to let a boy put his hand under your dress.'

After being given the facts in a light-hearted manner to avoid embarrassment, Mother changed the subject to powder and paint, letting Alice choose some discarded boxes of face powder and a lipstick that Mother had decided wasn't quite her. It wasn't long before the attic, which used to reek of musty old bread papers, oozed seductive perfumes: Evening In Paris, Woolworth's sixpenny bottles of Jasmine, Californian Poppy, Jockey Club and Devon Violets, all mixed up together.

On half-day closing, when Alice went home to Barnsley, she always went loaded up. Clothes that we had outgrown were welcomed eagerly and she never went without a basket full of groceries, free, for her mother. She was happy as a lark that she was able to help out, and wanted for nothing more.

One Wednesday she confided, 'I'm not bothered about going home really. I'd rather stay here with you lot. I only go to make sure me mam's all right.'

Alice had slotted in perfectly with us. We couldn't imagine life without her hysterical screams of laughter and yells of 'You Do!'

I don't know who was the saddest, Alice or us, that awful day when she burst into the house crying uncontrollably. She had been on her weekly visit home, and was looking forward to going to the pictures with Leslie that evening.

'Me mam's very ill, and the new baby too,' she sobbed, throwing her bag down on the couch and shuddering in utter despair. 'Me dad says I've to give me notice in, and I don't want to. Oh Mrs Taylor, what shall I do? I don't want to go and live there again. I don't want to leave you all. And my own lovely bedroom.'

There was nothing we could do to help, apart from telling Alice she could always come back and see us whenever she wanted. The week's notice over, she was inconsolable when the day came for her to leave us. Her brief flight of freedom was over. No more reading in bed until the early hours and no more privacy, even though that privacy was only an attic bedroom where mice played hide and seek. No more shrieking with laughter when commercials chased her round the kitchen table, and probably no more decent, appetizing meals. There wasn't a dry eye among us as she packed her little brown attaché case for the final return journey, stuffing in extras we insisted she take in her brown carrier bags.

A week later the postman brought a letter from Alice. 'Dear Mr and Mrs Taylor,' it read. 'Me mam passed away and now there is nobody else to look after the children but me. Thank you for giving me such a happy home. Yours sincerely, Alice.'

We didn't get another maid. The attic stayed as it was, ready for 'You Do!' if ever she managed to come back. She never did. I often wonder, many years on – Alice, where art thou?

CHAPTER SEVENTEEN

ALL CREATURES GREAT AND SMALL

The great advantage of living over the shop was that in wintertime Dad didn't have to turn out for work to wait for buses that never turned up, like lots of the villagers had to. But he had to turn out unexpectedly one freezingly cold night, all because of one of Mother's admirers, Ben Clay.

Besides being a big draw with all the commercial travellers, Mother had lots of followers among the animal population too. Besides Prince, our dog, and the seven resident cats – ostensibly kept to keep the mouse population down, but a lazier lot you've never clapped eyes on – we had a yard full of hens, all of which Mother had christened. Her special pet hen was a dainty, feathery affair named Black Auntie.

All the cats had begun life as strays. One, later named Pussy Bakehouse, spent the greater part of her time snoozing, not in the bakehouse, which had originally been her appointed working place, but draped round the base of our upright, daffodil-shaped telephone. It didn't take her long to worm her way into the kitchen and join the others. They enjoyed dreaming and snoring on the pegged rug before the fire when all

Audrey (Philip's future wife) and Ben Clay, with Major the labrador

the chairs were occupied by humans. When all of them were sprawled on the rug there was no way of telling what colour it was.

But to return to Ben Clay. Ben was the big old carthorse who was also very much alive to Mother's vivacious charms. Although Mother was a real coward where large animals were concerned, she made gods of the familiar ones who lived in the field over the broken-down fence at the bottom of our back garden, and ministered to their requirements daily, as long as there was a fence between them and her.

As well as Ben Clay there were three cows named – by Mother, not the farmer – Beauty, Sulky and Buttercup. The fence had been battered by the huge animals as they charged down for their daily titbit from Mother: stale loaves, Madeira and fruit cakes.

'Come on Ben, Beauty, Sulky, Buttercup!' she called, bearing an apron full of goodies.

'You'll have that damned fence down completely in a bit,' Dad used to complain. The only answer he received was a toss of the black hair and a derisory snort. It wouldn't be Mother who had to put it up again, so why worry? After 'keeping the band in the nick' with the farm animals, Mother popped back into the shop if one of her favourite travellers was there, or to whoop it up with the Vinegar man, who'd always fancied her. With both the animals and the reps, Dad warned Mother, 'You'll lead them up the garden path once too often.' She did.

One dark winter evening she was mending a few socks by the fire when the back door knob rattled violently. Mother believed in keeping doors firmly locked after the shop was closed for the night. There were no lights round by the back door, only the vast blackness of the field and woods beyond the garden. But on moonlit nights one could sometimes make out the shadow of a horse or cow moving silently along.

When the door knob rattled again, more insistently, Mother forgot her caution, thinking it was perhaps one of us who had forgotten our key. What a fright she had when she inched open the door! And what a good job there was a chain on too. Ben's huge brown nose butted her chest and his front hooves lunged forward, in a determined attempt to get over the doorstep and into the house. After all, he'd been encouraged enough.

With presence of mind born of sheer terror, Mother unceremoniously slammed the door shut in her perplexed suitor's face, and rammed home the bottom bolt for good measure.

Next morning she felt quite ashamed at seeing the rejected Ben, and Dad banged a few nails in the broken fence and hoped that it would last a while longer. It did, until the early hours of the next morning.

We were all four in our beds when the silence was shattered by the sound of clattering hooves. It sounded for all the world like Tom Mix and Trigger cantering on the path alongside the house. The danger was that in the middle of that path was a steep, unfenced flight of steps leading down into the bakehouse yard.

The horse could break a leg or even be killed if it fell down there. And it would be our fault.

In his nightshirt, Dad, now a corpulent seventeen stone, swung his feet over the edge of the bed on to the cold linoleum.

'I bet it's that damned hoss again,' he swore as he swished open the landing window.

Mother's voice, muffled from beneath the safety of the blankets, called out, 'You'll have to do something. It's pitch black outside. What if it falls down the bakehouse steps?'

'What if *I* do?' spat back Dad. 'It's your fault for encouraging the blasted thing.'

He fumbled into his crumpled trousers, hooked his braces over his shoulders, and clattered downstairs.

No sooner had he opened the back door than a rush of cold air swept upstairs, and Mother plaintively moaned, 'It'll kill your dad if it's charging back on the path as he's turning the corner. He'll be trampled to death – he shouldn't bother about it.'

Hilda and Major in the back garden

Philip and I dashed to the window and peered out. A gale-force wind was blowing and somewhere in the wood an owl hooted dolefully. Dad, hair standing wispily on end, suddenly appeared on the back garden path, looking like a poor man's cowboy and patting Ben's flanks, coaxing the horse bravely.

'Come on owd lad, there's a good boy. Back to your field, eh?'

Ben stepped carefully over the fence, which was lying flat in the garden, tossed his head and emitted a wild neigh. A few minutes later the back door slammed and Dad ran upstairs.

'Shove up,' we heard him say as he flopped back into bed. 'It's like bloody Iceland out there.'

There was another shock the following afternoon, before he had a chance to fix the fence properly. Artificial silk stockings were always easy to get in the back kitchen, stacked up in white cardboard boxes on the drapery shelves. So naturally, when Mother needed a new pair she simply took another lot from the Bear Brand box. That day she decided to wash scores of

Hazel and her mother with the new puppy, Major

stockings that had accumulated in her dressing table drawers. She pegged them out on the clothes line where they blew gracefully, like the disembodied beige legs of Ziegfeld chorus girls.

Some time later, Mother popped out into the garden to bring the dry stockings in. They were mere ragged stumps attached to a row of wooden gipsy pegs, and she arrived just in time to see the ample rears of her three favourite cows ambling contentedly back into their field, their hooves lifting delicately over the flattened fence, and their jaws munching on the remains of their afternoon tea. During the next few days we half expected to see Mr Clay, our milkman, measuring out beige-coloured milk into our jugs, but miraculously it remained a healthy cream.

CHAPTER EIGHTEEN

SATURDAY PENNIES

Although we had a shop, I was still only allowed the traditional Saturday ha'penny, graduating to a penny weekly spending money. No wonder I still have my own, perfectly good teeth.

In our grandparents' day Yorkshire children called sweets 'spice', pronounced 'sparce' by the more broad Yorkshire types. They made a glorious show in the shop; gleaming rows of big glass jars proudly arrayed on a shelf over the window display of seasonal goods. Shuttlecocks and battledores, whips and tops with packets of chalk, and skipping ropes with small handles or more expensive ones with huge bulbous handles and silver bells attached. Many children though, made do with old clothes lines for skipping. Bags of marbles dazzled the eyes of the boys, and no self-respecting youth went out without trouser pockets bulging with glass 'allays' and 'bulleys'. In springtime, when children's thoughts turned to outdoor games, there was a craze for yo-yos one year. We even had a few wooden hoops hanging up in the shop window round about Easter time.

The boiled-sweet manufacturers, Dobson's, was on top of the hill. Oh, the aromatic scents pervading the air when we passed by! Their speciality was Yorkshire Mixtures, coated with bits of sugar that looked like tiny bits of snow sticking to the boiled hard 'fishes', which were bright pink underneath. Brown- and white-striped humbugs, that were almost too big to fit into one's mouth at first, diminished with perseverance and no talking, until a point of humbug could fit comfortably in the gap between one's teeth. There were bright green lime drops, and pale pear drops, commonly known as gobstoppers, but my favourite boiled sweets were those fishes, with their wide fins and vacant expressions. Aniseed balls were also popular, and one got such a lot for a penny. Many a child experienced the awful sensation of a hard aniseed ball slipping down the throat unexpectedly, and sticking midway down for a few heart-stopping moments before a couple of extra-deep gulps pushed it further down the gullet. How pale we went at those times and felt to be almost a goner, vowing we'd stick to soft dolly mixtures in future, or jelly babies, all in neat rows in the white cardboard box, naked winter and summer alike, looking as though they were waiting for life to begin.

'Put us a lot of black 'uns in missus,' many children pleaded.

Sunshine flickering over the display shelf of confections made them appear even more delicious-looking. The counter was raised at the back to give small children a good view, while the head and shoulders of the assistant hovered, paper bag in hand, and waited for the ultimate decision. There were rows of shiny, ribbed liquorice braid. Some enjoyed it best by pulling thin strips off, while others preferred rolling it all up into a thick round wedge and stuffing the lot in their mouth, ending up with Charlie Chaplin moustaches and strutting round twiddling pretend canes.

Lucky bags were popular, in flimsy pale pink or lemon tissue paper, as was Caly – or was it Kali? – with a hollow liquorice stick pushed in the top of the bag to suck the bright yellow concoction up. Mouths turned a chemical yellow colour so it was easy to guess what the Saturday penny had been spent on. Those who had already eaten their sweets, or whose parents were out of work and couldn't afford to provide spending money, tagged along beside the Sweet Tycoons, eyeing the goods with woebegone expressions, moaning, 'Gie us a lick kid, go on, I'll be yer best friend if yer do.'

Fry's chocolate bars were a popular brand. In the kitchen was a long, framed photograph showing five little boys. Each expression suggested something about the forthcoming chocolate bar, something along the lines of Desperation, Expectation, Pacification, Realization and Acclamation.

For customers with a frog in the throat there were jars of herbal tablets, fawn-coloured and strong-tasting. There was a picture of a venerable-looking, balding, grey-haired man on the front, holding one to his mouth with a satisfied half-smile on his face.

'Don't eat too many at once,' Mother warned. They were supposed to send you to sleep if you did. We always stocked tins of Victory V gums, black as the blackest night, with a hollow in the middle where tongues could conveniently lodge. Boxes of Pontefract cakes vied for favour with ridged, harder Poor Bens and irresistible liquorice allsorts.

However, few sights on delivery day could better a newly-opened cardboard box full of sugared almonds. Refined customers, such as the schoolmistress and the parson's wife, were partial to a quarter of those for the weekend. How attractive they looked, smooth, pastel shades of pink, mauve and palest green.

When Grandad was in the shop and we lived in the little house down the bakehouse yard, I entered the shop like any other child, clutching my Saturday spending money and asking, always, for a 'halfpenny-worth of Riley's toffee rolls, please.' Grandad didn't show favouritism. He weighed them exactly, taking one off if they weighed more than they should.

Eventually Dad had machines installed on the shop's front walls for bars of twopenny chocolate, and also for Wild Woodbines and Craven A cigarettes. I enjoyed filling them on Saturday mornings when not cleaning out the henhuts or delivering grocery orders on the sack cart.

Saturday mornings were very Heaven in the thirties – well, they were if you lived at a grocer's shop. Mother never knew what it was to have to carry heavy shopping baskets, all our basic requirements being on the spot. She went about gaily singing all day long, flirting with all and sundry. 'Two Lovely Black Eyes, Oh, What a Surprise' or 'Have you ever been lonely, have you ever been blue, have you ever loved someone, just as I love you'; the very air we breathed was lightened when she was there. No wonder we were never lonely. Customers, travellers, nobody ever wanted to leave once they sauntered into Central Stores.

Mother, never too hot on mathematics (assistants jotted down prices in pencil on the counter where order books were placed), enjoyed washing shelves out on Monday, when the shop was relatively quiet; 'titivating the place up', as she called it.

I enjoyed tidying the fancy goods drawers, where reposed combs attached by rubber bands to pieces of white cardboard. Each piece of card had a picture of a coy young lady with marcel waves and Peter Pan collar, 'giving the glad eye' as mother called it. There were packets of fancy hair slides, some fashioned like little bows; tortoiseshell circular hair slides; packets of kirby grips, for those who preferred to water-wave their hair rather than go to a hairdresser; grey steel Dinkie curlers; Snowfire; Pond's vanishing cream; and sachets of Evan Williams shampoos – Brunitex for dark hair, Sta-blond for fair. Then there were bottles of Edwards' Harlene, bearing a picture of a lady with yards of wavy hair, who reminded me of a mermaid. We hadn't any customers who remotely resembled her. 'But you might if you bought a bottle,' Mother told them. I adored sniffing the various goods.

Later, cashing in on the appeal of Shirley Temple, we stocked bottles of Curly Top, a hair tonic specially for children.

But it wasn't all selling. We had to pay out for returned empty bottles, and when a lot accumulated there was many a banged shin on the crates waiting for the men to cart them away.

Little annoyances of life fade into nothing when real tragedies occur. Although few cars were in the village during the thirties, there were a number of accidents with horses and carts. Tom Ramsden's greengrocery business was run in such a manner, going round the streets with his wares. Waddles, one of the shop cats, was not as wide awake as in earlier days, and one Monday afternoon when the horse and cart were approaching, she decided to amble across to sun herself on the 'old ack' of the low-decker house opposite. Instead, the wheels of the cart went straight over her.

Customers were left standing as Mother, screaming hysterically, flapped about on the pavement shouting, as usual, for 'Joe, Joe'. Tom wrapped Waddles up in a sheet of newspaper, saying, 'I'll see to it.' Waddles was then put among the cabbages and cauliflowers on the cart and we never saw her again. Mother had a whiff of the smelling salts that she always kept in her handbag, and went inside for the customers to offer her comfort. This was the sign for someone to put the kettle on, and all to have a restoring cup of Typhoo tea and one of the iced buns from the tray in 'The Fittings'; a kind of impromptu funeral tea for poor old Waddles.

Martin Edmundson (the plumber's son) and Derek, friends of Philip, enjoyed playing up in the attic, reading comics and the latest edition of the *Magnet* and getting up to date with the escapades of Billy Bunter and Co. Sometimes they looked at Alfred's old photographic slides that were in a big mahogany box up there, and his camera, still with the black cloth hanging down the front. It was a wonderland up there, holding Alfred's glass slides up to the light and seeing scenes of many years ago.

Then Martin knocked up a wonderful trolley cart made from wood and cast-off pram wheels. One bright morning when ice was still on the hills and Tom's horse and cart were drawn up outside our shop, the horse with its head in the nosebag having a bit of a feed, Martin and Derek were trying out their vehicle, Martin with his back to where they were going, and Derek steering by means of an old piece of rope, facing him.

Somehow Derek lost control. Down they hurtled towards the stationary, unsuspecting carthorse. It's debatable who had the biggest shock – horse, Martin or Derek. With unstoppable momentum, trolley cart, Martin and Derek shot beneath the cart wheels and horse's legs, emerging pale but unscathed at the other side.

The story swept round the village like wildfire, too late to keep the tale from Martin's dad.

'You'll not ride on that damned thing again,' was the plumber's reaction as he took a hatchet and broke the contraption into bits.

Then came the craze for bicycles. Philip hadn't a bike, so Derek said he'd sell him one 'for ten bob'. A bargain. It was waiting for Philip when he returned home one dinnertime from Huddersfield Boys' College. There was just time for a quick tryout of the second-hand bike.

'I'll be back in a minute' were his last words before swinging himself on to the bike. The next we knew, Philip and bike were flying down past the shop, completely out of control. In a desperate effort to stop himself from hurtling further down the steep hill he managed to turn the handlebars into one side and collided with the lamp-post outside Edmundson's shop. The handlebars pierced his stomach. Mr Edmundson dashed out to try and help the badly injured boy.

Fortunately, Mr Davidson the insurance man, who had a car, had called next door to our shop. When Philip was brought in through the shop door, more dead than alive, one of his thumbs twisted right over, face white with agony, he was carried carefully round the crates of pop bottles and into the kitchen and laid on the black horsehair sofa. Mr Davidson offered to take Dad with Philip to the infirmary. During a five-hour operation Philip's spleen was removed; he also had a dislocated shoulder and thumb. It wasn't thought

Joe and John Hall, the shop assistant, sporting the latest in men's swimwear in the 1930s

that he would live. Dad lay on a table next to him giving a transfusion of blood. Mother and Dad stayed by his bedside throughout the night, while John, our assistant, slept at the shop to look after me.

I felt dreadful seeing Philip's other pals going about as normal, while Philip might be dying. All because Derek had put a rusty nail in where a brake block ought to have been, to save a few coppers or the bother of going to buy a new one. It was eight months before Philip was fit enough to return to the college.

He and Martin had both lived to tell the tale after their hair-raising experiences, and were later to tease those attending Band of Hope Temperance Meetings at the Sunday school. Standing outside, ready to run, with Leslie and a few other village lads, they bellowed a made-up song to the tune of 'The Soldiers' Chorus' from *Faust* – 'Beer, Boys, and bugger the Band of Hope.'

There was no badness or vandalism in any of them, just the evergreen renewal of youthful high spirits experienced by succeeding generations.

CHAPTER NINETEEN

BLUE SKIES ALL DAY LONG

Youthful spirits were usually in evidence when Dad organized the annual grocer's trip on a charabanc. Selected customers – those who could be relied upon to pay on time – were invited, and round about April they started bringing weekly sums to the shop to be put by in the nutmeg drawer for the chara trip. Anticipation was the thing, and not too many treats in one year. Otherwise people became blasé about them. Even in the mid-thirties not many could afford to take their families away to the seaside for a week, but a day was possible, especially if someone else kept the reins on the savings.

Almost without fail, on the big day itself the sun rose bright and early in a clear blue sky. Anxiously, Philip and I peered out of the front bedroom sash window for the first sign of the chara. Soon, the shop square thronged with laughing, joking customers, who raised a loud, vociferous 'Hooray, here it comes!' when the open-to-the-sky charabanc ground to a halt and the merry-eyed driver leapt out and thumped loudly on the shop door.

'Come on, Joe lad,' shouted his customers. 'Get thi shirt on. Gerra move on Hilda.'

Mother, flushed with an overdose of rouge and excitement, waltzed out, knocking imaginery bits of fluff from her braid-trimmed, long-waisted, navy-striped costume, adjusting the white fox fur round her slim shoulders, and putting on her best cloche hat.

A chapel choir outing in a charabanc. Among the trippers are (in the chara) Hilda and Joe with Philip, Tom Jessop (next to the man in the flat cap), and Wright Charlesworth. In front are Ella Lunn (in the beret), Arthur Priestley (the choirmaster, holding his trilby), Blanche Chinn (the Sunday school teacher, in the fur-edged coat), Harry Gibson (in the flat cap) and Alan Dyson (standing on the runner)

'Oh, what a handsome driver!' was her usual first remark, whether he could lay claim to that distinction or not, giving the laughing young man a playful flick beneath his chin with her kid gloves to roars of approval from the delighted customers. Everything augured well for a relaxed, joyous day out.

After a deal of good-natured bantering, spinsters and bachelors paired off on the back seat and we set off with a chug and a splutter, to the sounds of making early whoopee from the rear. Everybody waved frantically to other passengers on the other charas, yelling out endearments and cheering madly when we took the lead.

The chapel choirmaster, who bought a dozen jam and lemon cheese tarts every Saturday, didn't need much persuasion to stand in front and lead his 'dear friends' with a hymn first, followed by 'On Ilkley Moor Bah't 'at', 'Sally', 'The Man on the Flying Trapeze' and other favourites.

To me, in cotton dress, sandals, blazer and straw Panama, sitting next to Philip in his short flannel trousers, knee-length socks with coloured stripes round the tops, a blazer and schoolboy cap, it was like being in Heaven itself, careering along the summer roads to the seaside with all our customers and friends, especially with the nonstop concert thrown in. I adored Mrs Griffiths, the coalman's wife, singing 'Little White Gardenia' and thought how wonderful it would be in years to come when I'd be grown up and perhaps canoodling on the back seat with a handsome young man.

The ladies looked very smart with their coy, stiff waves and sausage-roll curls. Marcel permanent waving was within the budget capabilities of the middle classes then.

Sporty types, members of the local tennis club, wore tightly-belted fawn trench coats, with berets worn almost flat against one cheek, to give a racy effect. As the morning wore on, and spirits became bolder, Mother pinched the driver's cap and strutted up and down the aisle giving an impromptu version of 'Burlington Bertie', then 'Whispering while You Cuddle Near Me', to roars of approval from the others. Her vivacity appealed to the young men, who leaned out to grab the performer as she swayed provocatively past.

Most men wore their best clothes. Suits with knife-point creases; waistcoats sporting gold alberts with watch chains dangling across youthful middles; black or brown shoes polished with Cherry Blossom to a shining intensity, with more daring ones in two-tone brogues with punched holes across the toes.

Dad was anything but a 'flannel bags' chap when it came to special occasions. As organizer, he took particular care to distinguish himself. At the last moment, before boarding the chara, he plucked a perfect bloom from the rose bush to enhance the lapel of his grey worsted 'chapel suit'. Grandad's watch and chain adorned his expanding girth, while his black shoes shone splendidly. He carried the inevitable pair of grey kid gloves.

Sitting behind Dad, I loved to trace lines with my fingers along the furry velour of his best trilby hat. Most of the older men wouldn't have dreamt of wearing anything other than white shirts and stiff collars. Dark and striped 'union' shirts were

A choir outing to Windermere. Hazel and her mother are sitting in the centre of the picture, looking towards the camera. Tom Jessop, in the blazer, with his back to the railings, is also enjoying the trip

working attire only then. A few wore fancy knitted ties, with purple predominating.

The chara being open to the sky, there was no stuffy, smoky atmosphere to detract from the sheer carefree enjoyment of the day. Many smoked, but the smoke swirled upwards into the bright blue yonder. There were no such annoyances as blaring transistors either, to create discord.

Mother kept driver and passengers refreshed by handing round a huge bag full of mint imperials from one of the big glass sweet jars. She also had an assortment of everlasting sticks, with which she amused herself by trailing some over the one or two bald heads among us. She had filled other sweet bags with sugared almonds and big brown striped humbugs.

Someone invariably suggested, 'Give us a song Hazel and Philip.' Philip never did, not enjoying being in the public eye as much as I did. How well, or badly, I performed, mattered little. The pennies popped into my blazer pocket were in appreciation

Joe and Hilda Taylor, with grocers from all over the country, on a special visit to Cadbury Brothers Ltd, Bournville, 28 September 1938

A village trip to the sea-side, 1937. Hazel is on the far left, in her Panama and brass-buttoned coat. Philip looks equally smart on the far right. Hilda is in the fur-trimmed coat

of my not being sulky. 'All Things Bright and Beautiful', piously sung, brought in a decent haul.

The choice of where we went was between Blackpool, Scarborough and Morecambe. I liked Blackpool best, because on a chara one could always see it coming, with the Tower rising in the distance, almost within reach. It looked so much more attractive glinting gold in the sunshine than at close quarters. Like coffee smelt while outside the coffee shop, or fish and chips on the cold night air.

There at last, many of the younger ones shot off immediately in the direction of the Pleasure Beach, while others couldn't wait to hurl themselves on to the warm, golden sands, to be photographed with little shaggy donkeys. Fancy wearing best suits, even furs, and lisle stockings or artificial silk, with low-heeled, double-bar shoes fastening with a button, to fool around on a beach! Yet those girls of the twenties and thirties, Gladys, Lizzie, Nellie, Muriel, Hilda and the rest of them, were considered extremely fashionable, and it was quite obvious that their young men thought them the bee's knees.

The daring ones who had taken bathing costumes emerged

from beneath enormous bath towels in monstrosities with built-up shoulders – thick woollen costumes, the majority patterned with thick stripes in a dull red. The lower half fitted snugly, if itchingly, almost to the knees. How fortunate that the Grocer's Trip usually enjoyed perfect summer weather, for what a lot of drying those garments took afterwards.

Tables for lunch and tea were pre-booked at a high-class restaurant. The grocer's party was ushered to its places as though it were royalty. The small trader was a comparatively wealthy man in those days, and bringing all that custom to the restaurant deserved the utmost attention and respect. Dad always left a good tip.

Menus hardly varied from year to year. Everyone plumped for hot soup, then fish fresh from the sea, and it really did taste fresher, and lots of chips. There were plates heaped high with thinly-cut bread and butter, and all was washed down with cup after cup of lovely strong tea, with a grand view of the sea to go with it. Utter perfection! The only problem was who to sit by. I liked everyone, and each had a different brand of humour to lace the meal with.

There were potted palms in a corner of the restaurant, and a discreet trio playing tunes of the moment, which all added to the delightful atmosphere. Nobody seemed to faint or feel at all tired on that day. They wouldn't have dared. They wouldn't have got their hard-earned money's-worth if they had.

So everybody felt top-hole, and as the day drew to a close all joined together for an arms-linked final jaunt along the promenade, singing heartily 'Oh I do Like to be Beside the Seaside' before making their way to the chara parking place.

The journey home was even more boisterous, with balloons, Kiss-Me-Quick paper hats, sticks of brightly-coloured rock and tales to relate along the way. For me, a child then, there was the additional thrill of being out on the open road long past my bedtime, seeing the trees bright green on the outward journey, but now strangely different as dusk drew in.

Those grocers' trips were one of the highlights of our village year. For me, and all the others, there were 'Blue Skies, Nothing but Blue Skies, All Day Long'. Just like the words of the song.

CHAPTER TWENTY

A HOLIDAY AT AUNTIE ANNIE'S

There were usually blue skies and sunny days when I was dispatched to Auntie Annie's for a week of my summer holidays, but they weren't the idyllic blue skies of a real holiday. (We had two Auntie Annies – this one was Annie Brummit, a relation by marriage.)

Annie had no children of her own, so she liked my brother Philip and me to call her Auntie, as the next best thing I suppose. She came to our shop every Thursday, to spend the day socially. When you live alone, being invited out even to darn socks is something to look forward to, especially to a house and shop, where customers are constantly toing and froing. Some ladies look in their element with one of those mushrooms in their hand to assist darning, and a pile of dark-coloured wool by their side. Auntie Annie was one of them, perhaps because when her husband George passed on, the hole in her life was as big as some of those in Dad's socks, and filling them in helped fill in her loneliness as well.

Thursday was the day the fishmonger came round with his cart, so we always had fish, mashed potatoes, peas and parsley sauce for dinner with Auntie Annie. Then there'd be jam roly-poly or treacle sponge and custard to finish off with.

'How are you going on at school?' was the first question put to us by Auntie as Philip and I hurtled in through the shop doorway. We heard about who'd died since last week, and who was 'badly', and who preached at chapel last Sunday.

Annie Brummit used to spend Thursdays at
the shop, helping to mend clothes

When we came back again at teatime, Auntie Annie had piled all
the darned socks into a cardboard box and she was enjoying a cup of
tea and fish paste sandwiches to 'put her on' till she reached home.

'We'll see you next Thursday, shan't we dear?' Mother said,
wrapping a Madeira loaf and a couple of slices of bacon up for
Annie as a thank-you gesture. To Annie, darning was a labour of
love, while Mother detested it. Besides, Auntie Annie got *me* for
a week when school closed for the six weeks in summer in
exchange for the weekly darning.

The 'Thursday Auntie Annie' was gentle, sweet, inoffensive
and mild, never annoyed when the cats toyed with her wool, or
if our collie Prince left his rough black and white hairs against
her black dress as he pushed past her. Even so, it upset me that I
was singled out to spend a whole week of summer in her dark
stone cottage at the other side of town. My brother always
managed to get out of it.

'He will want to be playing football or cricket with his chums,'
Auntie Annie reasoned.

Well, so would I, but I couldn't be rude and say so. Not after all that mending she had done. There was always something going on at the shop. One of the cats giving birth, a commercial traveller chasing Mother round the biscuit tins, the gramophone playing hit tunes of the day – there was never time to be bored living at a grocer's shop.

Then the date arrived for my holiday at Aunt Annie's. Mother, Dad, Philip and I were invited to her cottage for Sunday tea. We all went to her chapel, then came the parting. Mother, bright and breezy as usual, told me to 'keep an eye on Annie', Dad slipped half a crown into my hand, and Philip grinned sheepishly as they went for their bus back to the shop. Tears stung my eyes as I tried to smile and appear excited and happy. Auntie Annie held my hand and we walked slowly from the chapel up the cobbled hill to her home.

Annie Brummit and her husband, George Harold, in the 1920s

In the downstairs room, on a dark shelf, was a *Chatterbox Annual*. It provided my sole occupation on rainy days. There was always one rainy day, though not many. Year after year I read that *Chatterbox Annual*. Rubbed out the crossword solutions compiled on my previous 'holiday' so I could do them over and over again, while Auntie Annie pottered about the cottage, keeping it spick and span. Auntie Annie sometimes unwound old jumpers and tried to instruct me how to knit with the horrid, wrinkly stuff. Occasionally, in a burst of unprecedented confidence, she allowed me to dust, but I was far too afraid of breaking any of her cherished trinkets to enjoy it. So I sat on the little black stool until my whole body and mind ached with weariness.

But it was my annual treat. A change. It would do me good. And Mother had said that I must enjoy myself. I've never yet fathomed how anyone can be ordered to do that, yet people still keep on saying it.

More and more ordinary families among our customers were finding it possible to go away for a few days during wakes week. You were considered a nobody if you stayed at home. Dad felt obliged to give our customers all-year-round service, and it was a bit of a problem finding somebody trustworthy to look after things, even if we only had a long weekend at Blackpool or Scarborough. He therefore thought that this annual week at Auntie Annie's was an added bonus for me. When I demurred, all I got was, 'Well, it's a change.' What use is a change if you don't enjoy it?

So there I was, stuck in that dark cottage for seven whole days. It felt more like seven years. On fine mornings, Auntie Annie, stacking the breakfast dishes into the stone sink behind the dark brown cupboard door, suggested cheerfully with that sweet, unchanging smile on her face, 'Run out and play with the other children. A bit of fresh air will do you good.'

The fresh air, alas, was lost amid the smoke from surrounding mill chimneys if it wasn't a wakes week. Then the neighbours' children had their own friends, and didn't, I thought, particularly want to know me. However, in those days we were taught obedience, so out I went and stood there, scuffing my heels into the grit of the recreation ground, staring at the rusting old rocking horse and see-saw. Stood there, thinking. Just thinking. First longingly about home and the shop, and all the hustle and bustle going on there, then, as big boys bullied and fought each other, and pushed girls off the swings, about golden sands, buckets and spades, rides on little grey donkeys, sea water splashing my bare feet, and the boisterousness of games of cricket with Philip and our friends. What was I doing here, in an alien land? It was only three or four miles away from home, but it might as well have been four hundred. There wasn't even a telephone in Auntie Annie's cottage. Only a big grandfather clock in the corner which boomed the hour, then fell maddeningly silent again for another sixty minutes. Back home there were never enough hours in the day to fit everything in. At Auntie Annie's there were far too many.

It's awfully hard work trying to look as though you're having a lovely time. The worst of it was, Auntie Annie did try to make it fun.

'Would you like to be a big girl now and fetch me some potatoes from the shop? Take my purse and basket, and when you come back there's a penny for yourself.'

She might as well have gone herself, for she stood at the cottage doorway, screwing her eyes up against the bright sunlight and shading them with a pale, blue-veined hand, until I re-appeared, trying to look excited at being allowed to go shopping

Happier times outside holiday lodgings in Blackpool, 1938. Hazel (second left) is sitting with other house guests

by myself. I spent my reward on aniseed balls; they lasted longest.

If it was fine, most afternoons Auntie Annie spruced me up to take me to the park. Clean white tennis socks, brown sandals, and a crisp cotton dress with knickers to match. That was, I suppose, in case I bent down for anything. Nobody would be able to differentiate between knickers and dress. Being respectable was the be-all and end-all for many village communities in those days.

In the park alongside the busy main road were half a dozen green benches to sit on it you got there before everyone else, a wire netting enclosure where a peacock strutted and held court, and a scrap of parched grassland bordered by well-behaved flowers, not like ours in the back garden at the shop, all mixed up with dandelions and thrown-out butter tubs, and the cats lolling about and squashing them down. A few old men with their coats off, shirtsleeves rolled up, braces holding up their trousers, postured on the bowling green to the admiration of wives and relatives with nothing better to do. Notices were liberally dotted around, warning everybody to 'Keep off the grass'.

Even though the sun may have been blazing down from a clear, cloudless sky, my world, bounded by the confines of the park, seemed as dead as a dodo. Yet it was there that Auntie Annie passed interminable afternoons, sitting tidily, unobtrusively on a bench, and chatting about chapel bazaars and the vicar's wife's scone recipe with other elderly, lifeless ladies dressed in dark shades of brown, grey or black, with touches of mauve or white at their necks. I was introduced to the row of faces with pride.

'This is my cousin Joe's girl, come to keep me company for a week.'

Then her listeners were regaled with a complete history of our family tree while I was coaxed to 'Play with your ball dear' or 'Go and have a look at the peacock.' I'd already seen it, lots of times, cocky thing that it was. 'But don't go on the grass!' a chorus of agitated voices called after me.

How dull everything was. I counted how many times I could bounce the ball on one spot. Threw it up. Paused to think about those far-off sands, and the constant merry tinkle of the shop door bell at home. Oh, how I wished I was at either one of them!

One of the ladies, a prim lady who looked as though she had a poker up her back, asked if I was good at counting. Why didn't I count the feathers in the peacock's tail, then come back and tell them? How I hated that peacock, though of course I wished him no harm. The feathers in his tail may have been bright, but without the right people and equally bright atmosphere, what good were they? Even the peacock, I thought, was probably another of those mouldy chapel ladies in disguise.

Tea at the cottage was invariably the same. Home-made bread with either lemon cheese or strawberry jam. We had the wireless on sometimes; *Children's Hour* or something like that.

We never went out after tea. Evenings were the worst, but at least they meant I was one day nearer going home. After another look at *Chatterbox*, and a digestive biscuit from the tin with a picture of a crinolined lady on the front, there was a cup of warm milk. I hated warm milk, especially the type with a skin across.

'Water will be all right,' I tentatively ventured one evening.

'Nay, now what would your parents think if I gave you water when you were on your holidays? They'd think you'd gone to prison.'

'That might be a lot more interesting than this,' I glumly thought to myself.

'I think it's time you went up now,' Auntie Annie said, on the stroke of eight. As I gazed at her, I thought how strange it is that people can seem entirely different in different surroundings. I

An older Auntie Annie with a group of friends (sitting at the end of the middle row)

liked her much better when she was darning socks in the back kitchen at our shop.

'I'll come in to say goodnight, and to hear you say your prayers,' she murmured as I wound my way miserably up the narrow twisting stone staircase to the tiny back bedroom.

I didn't care for the picture above my head of an ancient, bearded man, with soulful brown eyes upturned to Heaven as I lay on the starchy white pillowcase. But this was a Heaven that was sepia-tinted and awesome-looking in the slowly dying rays of the summer evening, so different to my idea of Heaven as shown by the picture of Jesus in Sunday school, with lots of children crowding round him.

The big, bow-fronted chest of drawers in the corner was only opened, I suspected, to bring out stiff, cold white sheets for wrapping dead people in. Perhaps they were waiting for Auntie Annie to be wrapped up in, when she was dead. I'd looked in the drawers once and seen pillowcases edged with thick crochet work, shapeless nighties and mobcaps, all smelling strongly of camphor.

When I'd said my prayers, with Auntie Annie joining in, I said my private prayers in bed, mostly praying that I could be taken violently ill and be hurried back home to the shop.

Then a changed Auntie Annie glided into the bedroom. She believed in early to bed and early to rise, and all those kind of mottoes. I always did feel more vulnerable in a horizontal position, but never more so than when confronted by a pale old lady clad from neck to toe in a voluminous flannelette nightgown, with no teeth in, and with her usually tightly-knotted bun of grey hair flowing unrestrained and all crinkly a long way past her shoulders. Slowly, with a sweet, religious kind of smile hovering round her anaemic-looking lips, she advanced. Stooping over me, she kissed me goodnight, the grey hair brushing my cheeks, while I had a close-up of the downy moustache on her upper lip. It took all my self-control not to scream out loud. But whatever would I have said on future Thursdays about my strange behaviour on my holiday if I had?

How I longed for Mother, and how I yearned for the sound of our radiogram, with 'Home on the Range' and all the other songs she loved to play on it. Instead I had the interminable silence of that room, followed by the soft rhythmic rise and fall of Auntie Annie's gentle breathing in the next room. After that Visitation it took ages to get to sleep, what with that picture watching my every move, hearing my every thought, and the unbearable knowledge that at that very moment people were laughing and jostling along seaside promenades.

Breakfast time again, and a boiled egg eaten with a thin spoon with an Apostle on the handle, and desperate thoughts about the day ahead. *Chatterbox*, the park, chapel ladies, the peacock.

Then at long last it was Saturday morning, and there came a knock at the door.

'Hello, anybody at home?'

Mother! Devon Violets flooded the air, and Auntie Annie came to life, exactly as she was on Thursday mending days. Beloved freedom, the treat was over!

The only person who had enjoyed my holiday was Auntie Annie, and the only drawback to my intense relief at being once again at Central Stores, among familiar faces, was the remembrance of Auntie Annie's final words, ringing loud and clear in my ears.

'Remember Hazel dear, I shall be looking forward to having you again next year.'

CHAPTER TWENTY-ONE

CHINKY'S FUNERAL

We loved all our cats, but my favourite was little hard-furred Chinky, so-called because of her yellowy, ginger and black Chinese appearance. A strange little creature, Chinky had walked in from no one knew where, with the unusual habit of sitting on her haunches and begging at the table, exactly like a dog. She sat on Grandma's lap while she listened to the records, and purred loudly as she was stroked.

None of the war news was, to my mind, as awful as the day when Chinky had a fit and died, as we were having tea one Saturday afternoon. Philip and I, heartbroken, put her in a cardboard box which we found in the drapery drawer, and Dad, who had felt too ill to go to the football match, told us to 'bung her in the drapery drawer' until the three days were up. I'd stipulated three days before we buried Chinky, just in case she came alive again.

At the appropriate time the funeral cortege moved out to the henyard to hold the service for Chinky beneath the old apple tree, the tree which shaded the graves of so many of our dead pets and hens. Philip, who had a strong baritone voice, and rather fancied his chances as an opera singer, took the role of singing vicar. While I, blinded by tears, dug the grave, he intoned the funeral rites then asked us all to join him in singing 'Oh God Our Help In Ages Past'. Then he said, in a voice as deep as Paul Robeson's, 'Dust to dust, ashes to ashes, and may our sister Chinky be given Eternal Life. Amen.' 'Amen,' we all solemnly repeated, then trooped back to the kitchen, not a dry eye in sight, for a restoring cup of tea.

Inside, Mother took a couple of boxes from the drapery

drawer, where there still remained a couple of boxes of 'Women's Outsize' bloomers from pre-war days, and decided to cut them up for dusters.

'I might as well cut these old pink knickers up, get rid of them and make way for something else,' she sighed, wiping the tears from her eyes.

Suddenly she gave a horrified scream, and rushed to the door.

'Joe! Joe!' she screamed hysterically. 'Chinky's still in that box.'

Bunny, the Flemish Giant, and Prince – two more much adored pets

'How can she be? Have you gone daft or what?' replied Dad, gulping down the last of his tea. 'You've just been out there with us to bury her.'

Nevertheless he went over to the cardboard box which sat open on the table where Mother had left it.

'Good God, what's happened?' he almost choked, going very pale. 'Philip, go and dig up that grave. You've had the wrong flipping box. We've buried a box of womens' pink bloomers by mistake.'

It made a good tale to relate to the lads 'over there' in our next airgraphs.

CHAPTER TWENTY-TWO

A WARTIME DELIVERY DAY

During the war, of course, everything was scarce or rationed but Mother still preferred to allow people to help themselves if Mildred (the girl who helped after John had been called up) was away ill, rather than bother serving in the shop herself. She wasn't interested in dishing out uninteresting objects like butter and lard, or fetching coal up from the cellar.

Jimmy, a chap from the new housing estate who was on the dole and too old to be in the forces, used to spend lots of his time doing odd jobs at Central Stores. He used to enjoy exchanging his services for a free glass of pop, a sit down by someone else's fire, and a bit of chit-chat with Mother and Dad. Once, however, he was in the cellar far longer than it ought to have taken him to bring a bucket of coal up. When he did re-appear he had mysteriously developed a very large chest. It really bulged beneath his thick striped union-type shirt and his waistcoat buttons had been loosened.

'Ah think ah'll get off home now then,' he muttered, wiping his coal-blackened hands on his old corduroy trousers, but Mother was too quick for him. Of course if she'd gone down for the coal it wouldn't have happened at all.

'Just a minute Jimmy,' she said, rushing at him and opening his shirt. 'You'd better put that soap back before you do.'

He'd packed lots of bars of soap against his hairy chest.

It didn't deter him returning though. Pickings at the shop were far too good to miss, and he was back again after dinner wanting to know if Mother wanted any help.

'Ah've been fast asleep on t'rug,' he announced, 'listening to t'wireless.' Just as if nothing had happened.

Indeed, everything was more or less undercover in wartime, including bars of soap. Whereas in peacetime shopkeepers displayed their wares as prominently and attractively as possible, enticement and sales being the keynote, during the war years most things were hidden away beneath the counters. Except for non-rationed goods, most shelves remained barren, while those of us living on the shop premises felt to be in a continuous state of siege. When delivery vans drew up outside the door dozens of pairs of avaricious eyes strained to see what was arriving. Curtains were drawn to one side, and anxious faces peered out. We could almost feel those unseen figures waiting to pounce as soon as the van drew away, sometimes even before the driver had time to clamber back into his cab.

Dad tried to outstrip these hopeful customers, non-regulars in peacetime who made a habit of going round every shop in the neighbourhood seeing what they could scrounge. He pushed the boxes hurriedly away in the back kitchen, or told Mother to stow boxes of cigarettes in the top cupboard. Then Dad, Mildred or whoever was serving assumed an air of innocence as they faced the inquisitors, who gave no time to check the goods off or ration them fairly before they pounced, demanding what they appeared to think were their dues.

'Owt tempting?' droned fat Mrs Cooper, elbows resting listlessly on the glass-topped counter. 'Ah've used all me points up, but yar Tommy'll be coming on Sunday, and t'grandchildren. Yer can't let us have a tin o' salmon and knock it off me next lot of points can yer Joe? Has t'cig man been yet? Oh well, if yer have nowt gie us a dozen jam tarts to be going on wi'.'

'If this flaming war goes on much longer we'll all be clammed to death,' grinned Mrs Brook, from a few doors down the road. 'At least it's keeping me slim.'

Her first priority was cigarettes. As long as she could get packets of Players and Cork-Tipped and even Pashas she was happy. She played the piano in clubs to earn money for them, and her favourite tune was the 'Sabre Dance'. You could hear her banging it out hour after hour, even into the early hours of the morning.

She enjoyed helping Dad in the bakehouse on his busiest day of the week, Fridays. And sitting round the big kitchen table with us at suppertime having fish and chips from the shop down the road, discussing whether there was life after death. Jimmy was always there too, and Mildred, and anybody else who happened to be around when it was time for a volunteer to nip down for the 'land and sea' (fish and chips). Dad always paid. It cost nothing, or didn't feel to, when it came out of the cash in the till.

Mother, of course, was usually out dancing. She had a new boyfriend now, who she'd met at the dancing class. He was a widower, and Dad had already vowed to swing for him. He was comforted somewhat by a local lady, about his own age, who now helped him in the bakehouse. He used to go to her house for meals sometimes, when Mother was at the class.

Mrs Holdsworth had ginger hair and was referred to by Mother as 'that ginger bitch' when she and Dad were having one of their frequent rows. But she was as nice as pie to her when they were face to face. Of course, when the delivery men turned up, it was such as Mrs Holdsworth who had first pick of whatever was available.

Because everyone was assured of the basic necessities, such as food, it was the non-essentials such as cigarettes and chocolate that caused near riots. How Central Stores was assailed when word went round that 't'cigs' had been, though life at the shop, and those who ran it, tended to be so informal and harum-scarum that it was known for the rations not to be sufficient to go round. Either Mother had casually taken too much butter for our use, or too much had been given out to sailors, soldiers and airmen home on leave, that Dad was in the embarrassing position of having to admit that there simply wasn't anything left for a regular customer.

Oh, the row that ensued that Saturday Auntie Annie, who used to live at the shop in the early, well-regulated days, came to tea and to collect her rations, only to be told that Dad hadn't any left. Philip was sent into town to the wholesaler's to see if they could

Joe and Hilda, *c.* 1945

let us have some in advance off the next lot. No wonder Dad's angina became worse with the strain of trying to accommodate everybody, and keeping a watch on Mother, to make sure she didn't take some of the goods to her latest paramour.

In the days leading up to delivery day, Mrs Brook adopted an alluring attitude towards Dad.

'I'll give you a hand in the bakehouse Joe, you've only got to ask. Anytime.' Then there was a sly wink, meaning 'But don't forget the cigs!'

On D-Day itself the cigarettes were speedily shoved out of sight. The whole month's quota would have been sold in the first five minutes otherwise. But you couldn't fool such a mistress of detection as Mrs Brook. She simply stood there in the middle of the shop floor, radiating delight and laughing throatily. Dad loved to tease her.

Some of the friends who helped in the shop with Joe and Hilda. Jimmy (standing on the right), 'What Ho' (with pipe) and his wife (centre)

'What is it you'd like madam? Half a pound o' tuppenny rice, half a pound o' treacle, Mix it up and make it nice, pop goes the weasel.'

'Don't be so daft Joe Taylor. You know damned well what I want. And I know where you've got it – underneath that counter!'

Then she dashed round and had a friendly tussle. Emerging triumphant, as usual, she stuffed the spoils into her capacious black bag.

'D'you know, one of these days I'll end up smoking old rope, or our Jack's old socks if they don't turn up on time,' she threatened, eyes glinting with pleasure at the thought of the long drags in store.

Some packets of fags were always kept back for when 'What Ho!' called at the shop. That was his nickname because as soon as he entered he called out in a jovial manner 'What-Ho!' He lived in a ramshackle caravan in the middle of a field with his common-law wife, and made a living by odd jobbing, poaching and generally 'knackling' for people who required his services.

'Gie us a bob for this,' he'd say, throwing a newly-caught rabbit on to the counter. 'It'll save thi meat ration, help it out a bit.'

Then he gratefully pocketed the cigarettes in exchange.

Like 'Old Mr Truelove', the artist, his was a simple kind of life. On summer evenings there was nothing he liked better than sitting on the steps of his caravan with Molly, the love of his life, pipe in mouth, glass of ale in hand, watching the rabbits hop and skip round about them. Goodness knows how he could slay them after that.

Sometimes 'What Ho!' had more than one rabbit, and if Mrs Brook happened to be in the shop when he was, he shouted, 'Catch!' and one went flying through the air.

'Gie us a kiss lass, and seal t'bargain,' he said. 'D'you know, we can hear thee thudding out on that theer Joanna o' thine many a night. Sounds just like the beating of a thousand African drums.'

CHAPTER TWENTY-THREE

STOCK-TAKING DAY

'All hands on deck!' was the call that everyone readily responded to on the first bright Sunday in March chosen for stock-taking. It was a day for daftness, jollity and 'mucking in'. The bakehouse in the little cobbled yard alongside the shop was whitewashed on the same day too.

Frank, Dad's boyhood chum, turned up in his oldest flannel 'bags' and flat cap turned back-to-front, as though the peak being at the back would somehow assist the bold swishing strokes of his whitewash brush.

Jimmy, our customer who was partial to soap from the cellar, was best at labouring jobs, such as heaving heavy objects away from the walls in order to clean behind them. Though shirking paid employment, he adored being called upon to do odd jobs. Turning up first thing in the morning, after Mass, white muffler round his throat, he directed operations in grubby striped shirt and corduroy trousers and clogs. If he was still hanging about at dinnertime he was automatically included in the invitation to the roast beef, Yorkshire pud and mushy green peas washed down with bottles of dandelion and burdock or Tizer from the crates in the shop.

Jimmy almost wished he'd not turned up one year though. Mother, in her scatty way, had emptied the vinegar barrel into an empty Tizer bottle, so that the barrel could be exchanged for a new one when the traveller called. By mistake the vinegary 'pop' found its way on to the dinner table. Jimmy was gagged after the choking dust of the bakehouse, and dying for a sup.

Hazel, aged twenty, 1947

'Here we are Jimmy, have a good drink,' encouraged Mother in her usual hospitable manner. She was supervising the huge black Yorkshire pudding tin, cutting the tasty puffed-up squares flavoured with chopped onion and dropping them on to the big blue willow-pattern plates.

Jimmy flopped down, opened the top button of his trousers and undid the string which helped to keep them up, then flung back his head greedily in anticipation of the feast. A huge gulp then Jimmy groaned and spat out the 'pop'. Mother nearly let go of the tin in her fright.

'What's the matter Jimmy? Isn't it nice?' she asked innocently.

Then a look of horror crossed her face as she remembered, and grabbed the glass from Jimmy's grasp.

'Oh, I'm sorry Jimmy. Don't drink any more, it's vinegar.'

Of course, everybody else thought it a great joke, including Jimmy eventually, who was given an extra square of pudding to take away the taste, and a packet of Wild Woodbines pushed into his waistcoat pocket to make amends. So it was worth it really.

Cigarette-mad Mrs Brook, who lived next door to the bakehouse, would come in to lend a hand and stay for dinner. She had loose-fitting false teeth that clacked as she ate and constantly threatened to drop out.

Everyone was like a child really, dipping into a big bran tub, not knowing what would emerge next. Every item in the shop had to be listed and counted: fancy hairgrips; 'invisible' hairnets; sachets of Evan Williams shampoos; Harlene hair tonic; nit combs (which created much hilarity as our helpers practised with them on each other); bottles of Carter's Little Liver Pills, which had probably been there since Grandad started the business all those years ago, but as there was no date on them we hadn't an inkling as to how ancient they were; lots of Beecham's powders; Fenning's Fever Cure; black and brown shoe laces; collar studs; a drawer full of forgotten stiff loose white shirt collars; all were counted, listed and dusted before being returned to their places for another year.

There were lots of dyes, which poorer customers bought to give a fresh spring look to faded dresses or curtains. Starch and Dolly Blue had a ready sale, as did donkey stones, all of which were kept close to hand in open shelves beneath the counter. We even stocked a few swimming costumes in all-wool, with built-up shoulders and thigh-hugging lower bits. Dad took one to Blackpool one year to wear when paddling in the sea.

Mildred recalls one summer afternoon when we took a tin bath into the garden and filled it with water to play in. 'You put a new blue woollen costume on and when you took it off all your tummy had turned blue.' So much for 'fast' dyes of the thirties! The only fastness was the rapidity of transferring the colour to your skin. I spent the rest of that afternoon showing off my newly-acquired pale blue belly to interested customers.

As the stock-taking Sunday wore on, Frank and Dad's faces and eyelashes became more and more caked with whitewash. The long-suffering cats became restless, hating the upset, wanting nothing more than everything to be back in its proper place, the pegged rug free from paraphernalia so they could resume their places on it before the fire.

Quite a bit of wildlife was found in the bakehouse to enliven the day. Jimmy was appointed to stand guard with the big coke shovel to nobble the occasional mouse or black beetle that sped across the stone floor when a flour or mixing machine was moved. He really thrived on that type of employment. He was in charge now, whereas in his last job in a mill he was the one who had nearly lost his life.

Having indulged in a jar too many one dinnertime, Jimmy was in high spirits bawling a popular ditty of the time above the noise of the machinery. 'Fall in and follow me, fall in and follow me,' and he'd literally fallen into what he described as a 'wuzzer' – head first.

It put him off legitimate work for the rest of his life. He had a brother who lived on the new council estate who shared his sentiments. Jimmy explained it by turning a gnarled forefinger to his head and making his eyes look like gobstoppers.

'Screwy, our Seth. Bonkers. But bonkers in t'right way. Gets free kip down at t'nut house. Too much oil in his can to work himsen into an early grave.'

All our helpers stayed on for tea. Mother was ringing the upright telephone extension handle one afternoon, to let those in the bakehouse know that tea was on the table, when Jimmy clattered into the kitchen dangling a newly-clobbered mouse by its tail.

'Wheer's them theer moggies o' thine? Ah've copt a titbit for 'em.'

That was one less item to account for on stock-taking Sunday.

Hazel serving Una Pearce in the shop, 1948

CHAPTER TWENTY-FOUR

THE LONG NIGHT

It seemed as though the worst that could happen had happened. After Dad had sent flowers to Mother, 'With Love, Joe', on the eve of their silver wedding anniversary, Mother had decided not to see Syd, her fancy man, again. She went round that very same evening to tell him, with Mrs Davidson for moral support. Dad, meanwhile, had sought solace with his own lady friend.

When the tall policeman called round at the house later that evening, however, we knew that Dad's attempt to patch things up and win back his wife must have somehow gone wrong. The policeman was flanked by Frances, who lived in the little house down the bakehouse yard and whose pale blue eyes were brimming with tears.

'It's Joe,' she finally blurted out. 'It's your dad . . .'. She couldn't go on and stuffed an already sopping-wet handkerchief into her mouth.

I leapt to my feet.

'What's the matter with him? What's happened?' I screamed, my pent-up emotions of the last few months bursting out.

'Keep calm then,' coughed the young policeman. 'Mr Taylor had a heart attack down at Mrs What's-her-name's.'

'Where is he now?' I sobbed.

'Take it easy lassie, take it easy. He's in no pain now. Isn't Mrs Taylor in? I think I'd better wait until she comes home,' added the policeman gently.

'I'll make some fresh tea,' murmured Audrey, picking up the kettle with trembling hands.

Mother's key finally turned in the back door at midnight. Her silver wedding day had begun. Philip couldn't keep the bitterness creeping into his voice as he confronted her with an accusing, 'Your husband is dead, you may be glad to know.'

Oh, how awful! How awful it all was. Her face first showed perplexity, then deepest despair. She half-stumbled across the floor, holding on to the table where, in happier times, Philip and I had sat at either end, while Dad wound a handle at one end to slowly reveal a big space where two extra wooden 'leaves' could be put in for when Grandad catered for funeral teas.

'Poor Joe, poor Joe,' she kept repeating, filling one handkerchief after another with big tears that seemed as though they would go on forever.

'I'll make another pot of tea,' Audrey patted Mother's shoulder. 'Philip's upset – he doesn't mean to be nasty – we're all upset.'

Through a marathon of tears and tea it dawned on us that the shop would have to be sold.

'*I* don't want it,' said Mother. 'I wouldn't know how to deal with food offices, and book-keeping or anything else.'

Then another thought struck me. Dad had arranged to cater for a couple who were to marry at the chapel in the near future. The usual procedure was that all the food, first made by him, was transported down the hill to the Sunday school for the wedding reception.

'What a mess we are in,' Philip sighed when I told him this. 'But we can't bother about it now. One thing's certain though, we're not turning it down. Catering's where all the profit is these days.'

We must each have sipped and gulped a dozen cups of tea while we sat in the kitchen waiting for the undertaker to bring Dad home. When the loud knocking at the back door came at 3 a.m., Mother leapt from her chair and ran into the darkened shop, so she couldn't see the men carrying the heavy coffin past the open door, and clumsily, bumpily, up the steep staircase.

'Where will they put him?' she gasped, not daring to emerge from the shop doorway, framed there, with the bacon machine in the background, a couple of the cats squirming round her legs, like some picture etched in time, waiting for the curtain to come down and someone to write 'The End' across it.

Her question was answered almost immediately by a shout from upstairs.

Joe Taylor, 1948

'Excuse me, where shall I put the – er – where shall I put Mr Taylor?'

Philip cleared his throat, trying to appear in control of the situation.

'In the back bedroom please.'

'That's where I sleep,' Mother faltered.

'I know,' my brother replied, meaningfully,

'I don't suppose any of us will get any sleep tonight anyhow,' Audrey filled the awkward silence, nudging her fiancé in an effort to stop him saying things that ought not to be said just then.

Mother stood there quivering.

'When will the funeral be, d'you think?'

Audrey put a reassuring arm round her shoulders.

'The undertaker will see to all that.'

'Can I sleep in a chair in your bedroom till then Hazel. I daren't stay in the same bedroom as . . . .'

The undertaker was a decent chap. His concern was no professional pose.

'Would you all come upstairs with me to see the body? He looks very much at peace. No, there's nothing to be afraid of Mrs Taylor,' as she flinched away.

My restraint broke again.

'But he doesn't want to be at peace! He wants to laugh, and live, and to enjoy his Silver Wedding today,' I argued.

'Oh dear, dear, dear, would it have been his Silver Wedding today Mrs Taylor? How unfortunate! Ah well, these things do happen. He worked very hard didn't he?'

We were following him up the stairs, turning reluctantly into the bedroom. I half expected to see Dad hiding behind the door, in his white baking apron, hair wispily standing on end, braces hanging lackadaisically off his shoulders. He'd yell 'Boo! How about that for a joke?' I felt the undertaker gently take my hand and lead me in. I faltered, drawing back.

'No. I don't want to.'

'Come along dear, do have a look at Dad.'

Dad? How could that person, so formally dressed in purple satin dressing gown – Dad had never possessed such a sissy thing as a dressing gown in his life – how could he be my Dad? Someone who showed no reaction whatsoever as those he knew best all stood round the open oak casket staring down. I noticed something else too, before the undertaker replaced the white cover over the set features.

'His face is blue!' I couldn't stop shivering, though the night was mild.

'That's his complaint – angina. That's what happens with heart complaints. But he does look peaceful, doesn't he Mrs Taylor?'

Maybe she was remembering that other September morning, twenty-five years ago, when she blithely enjoyed a rare bath in a proper bathroom in a neighbour's house, then showered herself with Ashes of Roses talcum powder, before putting on the white wedding dress and circlet of orange blossom to hold her veil in place. The honeymoon, the singing, the hit tune of the twenties:

> Wedding bells will ring so merrily,
> Smile awhile,
> And kiss me sad adieu,
> Till we meet again.

She couldn't reply. She simply nodded her head then turned to the undertaker with a pleading look in her red-rimmed eyes. He held her close for a few moments, as one would comfort a baby, then quietly closed the bedroom door behind us as we trooped back downstairs.

'Who won, Philip?'

Suddenly the match seemed ever-so important.

'We did,' he smiled briefly.

CHAPTER TWENTY-FIVE

GOODBYE
CENTRAL STORES

In the afternoon, about half-past three, the silver wedding party guests began to arrive. None of them were on the phone, and there had been no time to communicate with any of them. We hadn't a car either.

Alastair arrived after Frances had kindly lent him a bed for the night (with Dad laid out in the back bedroom, we were one bedroom short). Mr and Mrs Wood were next, with happy congratulatory smiles and beautifully wrapped presents. Then Dad's lifelong school chum, Frank, who slumped into a chair and cried uncontrollably.

'Oh Joe lad, Joe lad, me old pal,' he shook his head in disbelief, check cap pushed back from his forehead. It was our turn to comfort others. All stayed for tea, but were told to keep the gifts themselves, as mementos.

Monday arrived, and we opened the shop. Mother and Philip went to the solicitors and bank, and to order wreaths. Whenever I went to the bathroom I flew past the closed bedroom door in sheer terror, trying to blot out of my mind what lay behind it on the big double bed.

Next day, 21 September 1948, the shop was closed all day for the funeral. I went into town to buy a black hat, and thought I'd collapse as the assistant chattered brightly while I decided on one with a face-covering veil with big black spots; they might hide some of the tears and anguish. Each post brought letters of condolence, many from firms Dad had dealt with.

The scent of chysanthemums at home was overpowering. Wreaths of them lay in the bread trays, and in 'The Fittings'. Some came from wholesalers who had known Dad since his boyhood days, while others came from commercial travellers who had been friends as well as business associates.

At half-past two the undertaker and his assistants went upstairs to carry the coffin down into the kitchen for anyone to have a final glimpse of Joe, the village grocer. Then the lid was fastened down for the last time and Dad made his silent farewell to all the fun and laughter, tribulations and tears that he had known at Central Stores.

The sun shone brilliantly as the sad procession wound its way slowly down the hill, and neighbours and customers on the route paid their final tribute to a well-loved friend. Caps and hats were taken off as we passed, and one or two tearful women lifted their hands in a gesture of farewell. It must have been like a replay of the scene thirty years before, when Alfred was borne down that same steep hill to his final resting place in the chapel graveyard. It seemed incredible that my Dad was going to be lowered into that deep yawning dark earth, to lie forever in silence with Grandma and Grandad, his sister Annie who he had never known, and to be reunited with his brother Alfred after all the turbulent years.

Had they been wasted, all those years? Was life itself a waste, for all of us? The answer came in a strange way, as we tried to eat the usual boiled ham tea in the Sunday school afterwards.

'Ee,' sighed old Lizzie Wainwright as she poured tea from the big urn. 'Ah shall miss him. He did make some grand jam tarts.'

If we can all go to Heaven, or wherever it is we go to, and someone somewhere misses us for something we have done to bring pleasure to their life, then our lives will surely not have been in vain.

Once the funeral was over, thought had to be given to what I would do, and where I would live, when the shop was eventually sold. Everybody else was safely fixed up but me. Philip was established in his banking career, engaged to be married, and was welcome to stay at Audrey's home at weekends. Syd's offer of marriage to Mother apparently still stood, despite what she had

Philip and Audrey, *c.* 1948

or had not said to him on the evening of Dad's death. So she had somewhere to go when all the loose ends were finally tied up. But where could Spitfire, Hurricane, Cheeky, Ginger, Pussy Bakehouse, Major (the lovable black labrador we bought when my old pal Prince died) and I go? I'd thought about joining the WRNS, but dismissed the idea because I didn't think they'd accept five cats and a dog besides me. I'd toyed with the idea of living with Mother and my stepfather-to-be, more out of desperation than enthusiasm. But for the time being, all my energies had to be directed to dealing with the shop, making it appear a desirable residence, polishing up the old furniture, keeping the counters and shelves clean and tidy, putting down mousetraps all over the place, hoping beyond hope that when prospective buyers came they wouldn't be put off by squeaks and strange rustling sounds along the shelves.

Mice weren't as frightening in the daytime as at night, and I lived in mortal fear of having to sleep in that house and shop entirely alone. Obviously Mother didn't relish the idea of her new husband and me living beneath the same roof, so she suggested I could live with his old widowed mother, in a part of the town I didn't care for at all.

I was desperately worried. Part of me wanted the shop sold quickly, so we could all get on with the rest of our lives, but the other part of me dreaded it. It would sever once and for all my last links with what had been a safe, secure existence. If I didn't enjoy a job, I knew I could throw it up and live at the shop without any worries about where my next meal was coming from. All that would soon be over.

By mid-October Mother was gradually winding down normal life at the shop. Most of the time she was living at her new home, and her wedding was fixed for November. She had the carpets lifted from the upstairs rooms and removed to her new abode, and life at Central Stores became a miserable affair.

Mother put everything she could come across into the shop to be sold off. There was a constant sale of books, ornaments, chairs, even some of the old cardboard boxes from the drapery drawers, filled with old-fashioned shirts and a few forgotten flannelette bloomers. It's a wonder she didn't put price tags on the cats.

Oh dear, the cats — we all secretly worried about their future, but no one actually voiced those fears. As long as the shop still belonged to us, it was their home. Perhaps whoever bought it would take them too, as part of the goodwill that people were always talking about, like some people leave carpets and curtains for new owners.

CHAPTER TWENTY-SIX

GOODBYE TO THE CATS, THE SHOP – AND ALL THAT

One morning Philip had a rude awakening. He had stayed overnight at the shop to attend to a few business arrangements. I was up first to take his breakfast to bed before opening the shop. One of the travellers had made an appointment to see us with a view to buying Central Stores.

'I'm absolutely whacked with it all,' Philip puffed, handing me back the breakfast tray and snuggling back between the blankets. 'You're getting better at cooking. I might even employ you one day.'

Five minutes later the shop door burst open and a couple of hefty-looking fellows came in. A huge removal van had drawn up outside.

'We've been asked to collect a Put-U-Up bed, a mirror, and a radiogram by Mrs Gregory,' one of them said.

I stared at them, unable to say a word. Mrs Gregory was Mother's new married name, and she had never told me about this latest event, and certainly Philip, asleep in the bed upstairs, had no knowledge of it.

'You'd better follow me then.'

I led the way.

'These men have come for your bed Philip.'

I tugged the bedclothes which were cosily round his neck.

'I'm in no mood for any of your stupid jokes,' he mumbled, without opening his eyes.

One of the removal men spoke.

'This is the correct address, Central Stores, isn't it?'

Philip shot up in amazement, pushing the dark wavy hair away from his furrowed forehead.

'What the devil's going on now?'

'Sorry to disturb you like this sir,' apologized the little fat chap, 'but we'll have to hurry. We've a few more jobs to do before dinnertime.'

Philip stood there in his bare feet, clutching his pyjama cord round his middle, looking like a better class of convict in his green- and white-striped outfit. The couple then took the blankets from the bed, placed the pillow on a chair, folded the Put-U-Up neatly, and set off with it down the stairs.

'I'd been hoping to store that at Audrey's until we get married,' Philip complained. 'The flipping radiogram too.'

I didn't say anything, but wondered where I fitted into all this. Where did I have to take any of my possessions? He had already taken all those lovely records I used to love to hear, and the books and encyclopedias that had belonged to Grandad. They would be worth a lot of money. All I was supposed to do was to 'keep the ball rolling' at the shop, it seemed. Without pay too. I couldn't see about getting a job until the shop was sold either. I was trapped for the time being.

Apart from all that, there was still the emotional trauma of Dad's death, and worrying about having someone to stay with me every night. The place was so bare and empty now that my footsteps sounded heavy on the wooden floorboards, devoid of carpets upstairs. If I tried to sleep there by myself I knew that I'd be awake all night long, listening to phantom voices and, probably, footsteps from the past. The deep silence contrasted sharply with the bustle and laughter of years gone by. The record sessions, doors slamming open and shut as Dad kicked them open with his foot when coming in with a tray on top of his head, and the delicious moments of Christmas morning when Philip and I used to scamper downstairs after opening our stockings to see the 'big' presents on the kitchen table downstairs.

I remembered the thrill of opening a copy of *Schoolgirl's Own Annual* one year, given to me by Lyon's tea traveller; pictured in my mind's eye old Alf, the Yeast Man, and all the others who seemed to want to do nothing better than come to Central Stores for a gossip. Now it seemed that nobody wanted to be there at all. They had all gone.

But I was forgetting. There were still some of the cats left.

One morning my friend Mavis telephoned, full of apologies.

'Will you be all right by yourself tonight kid. I'm afraid I can't make it. Mother's not well.'

There was nothing I could say but yes. Then, as soon as I replaced the receiver, I burst into tears. I was terrified. I was sure that Dad's ghost would rise from that double bed and come floating eerily into my little bedroom, and the mice would turn out in droves, and nibble me to pieces.

Not long after, Mother's voice sang out over the telephone.

'Hazel? Syd wants to know if you'd like to sleep here until you get fixed up somewhere.'

The unexpected kindness made me blubber more than ever.

'Thank you very much. Thank Syd too. But what about the cats? And Major? I can't leave them here on their own. There'd be cat dirt all over when I came back in the morning, and I've more than enough to cope with as it is.'

There was a pause, then her voice continued.

'Do you think we ought to phone for a vet?'

I cringed. It was as though someone had kicked me in the chest and I couldn't catch my breath.

'Well, I know it's awful, but the poor beggars are too old to settle anywhere else but the shop, and there isn't enough room for them here, at a private house. I'll get Syd to make arrangements with one then, shall I? I wouldn't be able to ask him – the vet I mean – I couldn't stand asking him to – to –.'

Our phones went down simultaneously as we couldn't continue talking for crying.

Every customer who appeared during the next hour was asked

half-heartedly, 'You wouldn't like a few good mousers would you?'

But really I didn't want them to go anywhere else. What if they weren't as well treated as they always had been at the shop? What if they were turned out at night-time? Nobody seemed to want anything nowadays. The traveller hadn't bought the shop, and I was beginning to feel as though I was existing in a kind of no-man's land. Then the shop door tinkled and Mother came in.

'I've brought some sandwiches and chocolate eclairs for our dinner,' she smiled wanly. 'Don't let Frizby Dyke see us eating them or he'll be mad that we aren't eating his honey-cakes.' (Frizby Dyke was our nickname for the new baker we'd employed.)

How little it takes to lighten the heart, when it has been down in the depths for so long! The sight of someone familiar, who belonged at the shop, and the thought of those chocolate eclairs was almost enough to make me feel light-headed.

Then came the bad news. Mother's face took on a very 'worked-up' expression.

'Now Hazel, we'll both have to be very brave. The vet is going to come at two this afternoon.'

Cheeky, Spitfire, Hurricane and thin-as-a-lat Pussy Bakehouse stirred on the rug. It was dinnertime for them too. Pussy Bakehouse must have been like those always-slim women who eat what they like but live on their nerves. She had a voracious appetite, but her striped body never put on an ounce of weight.

'Have they had anything today yet?' Mother asked, pale as a sheet of cap paper beneath her rouged cheeks. 'I'll open a couple of tins of salmon for them then. Oh dear, isn't it awful having to do this?'

She turned away from me as she began to open the tins with the can opener.

'Don't cut yourself,' I warned.

I couldn't stand anything else happening. I saw the tears plopping on to the old sideboard and into the opened tins as she tried to muster enough courage to dole the salmon out on to saucers and put them down by the fire.

Cheeky waddled up to the saucers, ear bent over at one side, legacy of some long-forgotten fight. Spitfire and Hurricane dawdled up, still full from the milk and sardines I'd given them earlier. Pussy Bakehouse dug her claws in and out of the pegged rug rhythmically as she grabbed bits of salmon into her mouth. Mother and I watched them, mesmerized.

'I think the best thing will be to get them all into the cellar and keep the door shut. If we let them stay in here and the baker comes in they could easily shoot off into the fields,' Mother said.

Instinctively, we picked them up and each put two on our knees, stroking them in turn. Major seemed to understand the situation, and strolled up to nuzzle them too. The shop door bell tinkled. The cats sprang down and dashed to the saucers again, licking them clean.

'Close the door quickly,' called out Mother. 'We mustn't let the cats get out.'

Mrs Brook sauntered into the kitchen, cigarette drooping between finger and thumb, humming her favourite 'Sabre Dance', swinging her narrow hips from side to side as though she were a belly dancer.

'What's up with them?' she wanted to know.

'They're having to be put to sleep,' Mother explained, wiping the tears from her eyes. 'The vet promised he'd be here about three, and we'd to make sure they were all here when he arrived.'

'He promised it won't hurt,' I assured Mrs Brook, who's face by now showed an expression of disbelief.

'Good Heavens, Central Stores without cats?'

She made a gesture of hopelessness, stubbing out her cigarette in a plate on the table.

'Aren't you having a packet lately. Still, what else can you do?'

'They wouldn't settle anywhere else,' I sniffed. 'They're part and parcel of the fittings – like the resident mice.'

Mother was getting edgy.

'I daren't go with them into the cellar, but it's getting time.'

'Have you a drop of milk handy?' said Mrs Brook. 'I'll put some into the saucers and coax them down with me. Don't worry, I'll stay with them until he comes. Poor things. Come on Pussy, Pussy Bakehouse. Cheeky. Come on love, with your Aunty Brook.'

Down she went, the cats lolloping after her. Both Mother and I were verging on hysteria.

'I wonder if this is how gaolers felt when they had prisoners down in dungeons in olden times?' I said, trying to lighten the situation

'We could keep the bolt on the cellar door and Mrs Brook would never be seen again,' Mother replied, bending down to pick up the saucers.

I glanced at the clock on the mantelpiece. The hands pointed to two.

'It's time,' I said, heart beating like a sledgehammer.

As though on cue, the door bell tinkled again. Mother shot off upstairs while I went into the shop to confront our cats' gentle executioner. He looked, I was glad to see, very much like Dad: tubby in green check Harris tweed, with kindly blue eyes, and a firm handshake across the glass-topped counter.

'Don't bother to say anything. I know exactly how you must be feeling. But it will all be over in a matter of seconds. They will simply go to sleep and won't feel a thing.'

He indicated Major, who had gone round the other side of the counter to investigate.

'This chap too?'

'Oh no,' I managed to stammer. 'Only – only the cats.'

He followed me into the kitchen, and I pointed to the cellar door before blundering upstairs to Mother. Holding hands tightly we shut our eyes and began to mumble a prayer.

'The Lord's my shepherd, I shall not want. He maketh me to lie down in green pastures,' Mother began, then I continued fervently, 'Dear God, please, oh please don't let it hurt my Spitfire, Cheeky, Hurricane and Pussy Bakehouse.'

'And let Joe be there to welcome them,' finished Mother, as she went across to the wardrobe for more handkerchiefs and a bottle of brandy which was hidden away in one of the compartments. 'Have a sip of this, it will make you feel a bit better.'

We heard the shop door bell a few times, but neither of us attempted to go down.

'Mrs Brook will see to the customers,' Mother said. 'She knows what to do.'

Then all was quiet until a voice called out, 'You can come down now Hilda, Hazel. It's over. He's gone.'

She had a teapot of freshly-brewed tea on the table for us and had set out a plate full of Fox's ginger snaps.

'Ever so gentle he was. They all went to sleep so peacefully, one after the other.'

'They aren't down there still are they?' Mother glanced apprehensively towards the closed cellar door.

'No, he took them away with him. Come on now, drink up. It's all for the best you know. Most things are.'

Then Mrs Brook burst into tears and Mother quickly handed her a couple of new handkerchiefs from out of a box in the drapery drawer.

'Here, take these.'

Then she disappeared into the shop and came back with a couple of packets of Players. Mother was in her familiar role of Lady Bountiful again, gratefully handing out gifts for services rendered.

'Thank you very much for all you've done. I honestly don't know where we'd be without some of our good customers!'

'It might seem silly,' said I munching a ginger biscuit, glad for a semblance of normality once more, 'but does the pegged rug look to you as if it's weeping?'

Mrs Brook looked at it, then got up and lifted a corner.

She nodded her head.

'Yes, yes it does. I know what you're meaning. It'll be lost without 'em for a while.'

She sat down again and sighed heavily, gazing out of the big window to the green fields beyond, then fumbled in her crocodile handbag and brought out the new packet of Players. Slowly she extracted a cigarette and lit it with one of the tapers we kept in a tin in the fireplace corner. Mrs Brook inhaled deeply, allowing smoke to curl lazily into the air above her head, then screwed the cellophane covering into a tight ball before chucking it into the blazing fire. After a long silence, when we all felt to be recovering some of our lost composure, Mrs Brook began to sing softly:

Joe and Hilda on holiday at Butlins, Filey,
1947

There'll be bluebirds over,
The White Cliffs of Dover,
Tomorrow, just you wait and see
There'll be love and laughter and
Happiness ever after . . .

She forgot the next words and hummed the rest.
'Oh yes,' she went on, taking another sip of her tea. 'We'll all
meet again I suppose, one fine day.'
Mrs Brook blew another vapour trail into the kitchen.
'Yes, one fine day, God is good.'